DESERT WINDOWS

DESERT WINDOWS

By

Eddie Doherty

DIMENSION BOOKS
Denville, New Jersey 07834

Published by Dimension Books
Denville, New Jersey

Copyright © 1977 by Madonna House

CONTENTS

FOREWORD

Eddie and I

by Catherine de Hueck Doherty

It isn't easy to write about Eddie's *Desert Windows*! So many times I have crept quietly and looked out into what he saw so clearly there. For me it wasn't too clear, and again, it was.

It was a strange marriage that Eddie and I had, but a very pleasant one. No wonder the windows were always stuck though! How could it be otherwise. Our love-making, believe it or not, rated a book called *Tumbleweed*. After finishing each chapter Eddie would ask me if I wanted to marry him. I finally did.

But then, what happened? The windows were surely stuck! We took vows of poverty, chastity and obedience since I was the foundress of an Apostolate that called for such vows. It is on this chastity business, my friends, that the windows got stuck again and again and again!

But it was important that they remained stuck because in our age of free love (is it really *free* love? and is it really *love*?) someone had to carry the cross of chastity in unusual circumstances, and ours were certainly unusual. So the window stuck again and again, and yet they were wide open when you come to think of it. Hundreds of people came in through those windows asking us how we lived that way and why. What was it in us that called us to this life? All I could say, and all that Eddie could say, was what we said to each other when we looked at each other: "We were in love with God, and those who fall in love with God do the strangest things in the world." I guess ours was a strange life.

PREFACE

It was mid-July, 1969. We were sitting side by side on the top of the Mountain of Beatitudes, in the very heart of Galilee, land of the Lord. The "Lake of the Singing Harp," Lake of Genesareth, stretched to the far horizon. A lazy air descending from the Golan Heights tickled its surface. The ebb and flow at the shores were drunk with the hazy atmosphere.

We were silent. Heavy with the rising heat of the desert we could but listen. One does not need words to feel alive, to feel a presence and especially His presence. The Presence of the Lord was as velvety as a prayer. Only a breeze was stirring and we listened to His voice: "Blessed are the humble . . . Blessed are the kind and merciful . . . Blessed are the pure of heart . . . ." The tall palm trees swayed like the murmur of lovers. Birds fluttered around. Not singing! They were learning a new melody. And the Lake? The Lake was humming the ever new story that happened two thousand years ago. Nothing could stop the murmur of His voice to fill our hearts: "Happy and Blessed are those who strive for peace . . . How wonderful it is when you are lied about because you belong to me! Be happy about it! Be very glad! Dance for joy because the Kingdom is all yours!"

Edward Joseph Doherty, my newly ordained deacon, was listening too. He was watching the desert creatures coming to life. The desert was warm. It was bright. It created visions. It was a window to heaven. And everything was full of angels. The Irish Doherty was caught up into their dance. His blue eyes, his face of milk and honey, his deep-penetrating look of the lover, his tall-strong stature, every vital breath in him was aglow with an inner flame that made him look taller, purer, strong as a diamond, tender as a mother. He uttered a prayer. I did not hear. I sighed clearly for him to hear: "Blessed are the pure of heart!" He echoed: "Yes, my bishop, I see him!" Was not this his first desert window from where he saw God, talked with God, played with God, cried and laughed with God? It is all in this book.

I first met Eddie Doherty in 1958 in Madonna House. It was at "tea time," as the four o'clock family gathering is called here. I had just received my cross inscribed "Peace and Love." I was not a full member. Full membership is for those who give, for those who fully live, for those who are ever attuned to the voice of "love and peace." I became that day a receiver of these riches. Eddie kissed me. He hugged me and smiled at me. He said some kind words of joy. My eyes and ears carried him to the depth of my being. I had found a man, strong, open, simple in his greatness, humble in his fame. In my effusive and spontaneous Lebanese way I invited him to come to Alabama. I was a pastor in Birmingham. I had a large airy rectory. The invitation was repeated. It was insistent. One year later Eddie Doherty came and spent a month in my parish. Until my ordination as Archbishop of Galilee in 1968 he faithfully kept that yearly visit.

What a blessing it was for me and my parishioners. Year after year young and old waited for that visit. I shared with him my priestly life. My joys and sorrows, my triumphs and failures were his own. He came to know my parishioners by name. My rule of life in that parish was that four families should be visited every day. He shared the rule and was more joy and more consolation to everyone. The rich and the poor and the sick and the energetic children received both of us with the same hug, with the same smile, with the same expression of love.

My parishioners loved to hear him talk about God and especially about the life of his Madonna House "boys and girls." I even invited him to preach on the Sundays he was with us. The event was, naturally, reported to the bishop. At that time a layman could not preach from the pulpit. The angry fulmination of the bishop came always after Eddie had gone home. The next year the incident would have been forgotten. And the preaching would go on. For a whole month every five years Eddie Doherty was a preacher in St. George Church in Birmingham, Alabama.

A real priest knows that he cannot teach God. All a priest can do is to help others to have an experience from which springs admiration and awe of God, of life and of creation. Eddie was such a man. He was a priest all of his life, even as a newspaper man, running the streets for news, roaming the highways for a piece of life. In his books *Love Letters to Almighty God, Tumbleweed,* he always was an announcer of God's news, of good news, carrier of the Gospel of Christ, helping others to have a religious experience and sprinkling their way with light and life and courage. He was a priest before ordination. I can say for myself as a priest and as an archbishop that Eddie Doherty was the one to bring me into the realization of so many experiences that put me into an orbit of awe and admiration of God, of life, of love, of my brother, of this world, and of whatever is in this world. To me Eddie was always a priest of God, which made it an awesome privilege to place my hands on his head and consecrate him at seventy-nine years of age a priest forever. And so today it is a great and awesome privilege to praise and bless Father Eddie Doherty, the first priest I ordained, the first fruit of my fatherhood as a bishop. *Desert Windows* is the explosion of a priest's heart and soul. Light and radiance spring from it. Light and radiance spring from every page of this book. It is the singing heart of a priest.

When the infant Doherty became a boy he took off the infant wrappings and donned the trousers of a youth. It was a new life, a new discovery, a new celebration that followed him everywhere. When he became a man he donned the strength and the pride of a man. A great enthusiasm drew his Irish generosity for God to the monastery. Eddie thought to become a priest. When he discovered the face of womanhood, that same enthusiasm plunged him into another river of life. He put on the garment of marriage and donned the vestment of fatherhood. When he lost Marie, his wife, rebellion took over his soul. Man always seeks the Infinite, and Eddie rebelled because for him Marie represented the Infinite. But Eddie Doherty was a giant. With a newly discovered courage and enthusiasm, he spread his wings again: the wings of the eagle that never give up. He donned a second wedding garment. Mildred was a delight, a heaven and a security of life and love. An accident took her away. And the wings of the giant broke again. Rebellion became a storm, and the storm raised for him new challenges.

A Russian woman, a refugee of the first world war, a stranger in a strange land, gave Eddie a new vision of life by giving him the fullness of her love. Eddie married for the third time. Baronness Catherine de Hueck, mother of the poor, the destitute and the down-trodden in Harlem, New York, and in the Chicago Friendship Houses, became Mrs.

Doherty. Paradise was regained. Paradise sang and danced in every word Eddie Doherty will write until the day of his death. *Desert Windows* is simply the nectar of it all. He sings in it. He inspires. He opens visions and radiant dreams.

Eddie Doherty was born to be a lover and his love had no limits. Blessed are those who live and who love. He drank of love with joy. He ate of love with pleasure. As he worked with boundless enthusiasm, he loved with boundless enthusiasm. And as he gambled with life, he gambled with love. He loved. And he lost. He loved again, and he lost again. He loved a third time, risking everything that he was, everything that he possessed, all of himself, past and future, and he became poor for the sake of the poor, landless for the sake of the destitute, and childless for the sake of the Kingdom. He gambled his life and emerged a glorious victor. His poverty clothed crowds of naked and fed untold numbers of hungry. His vow of chastity that made his bed cold and lonely gave birth to countless children warmed at the rays of his love. Totally powerful in utter obedience, he acquired the richest of all riches in total self-giving in the Madonna House Apostolate.

Blessed is the man, blessed is the priest who abandons his own life to multiply it in others. Eddie was that priest and that man. Winner and loser, saint and sinner, a womb of superstition and faith, a genius in giving and receiving, always hugging close to the ball of the earth for life and for being. Every page of this book will distill and exude what life and love can inspire.

The priest is life, light and radiance and that is what we discover in *Desert Windows*. That is what we admire, that is what makes us stand in awe. The priest is indeed life, light and radiance, but soaked with tears, and drenched in suffering. Blood is life, and it is the most significant symbol of life. The sprinkling of blood is a seed and diffusion of life. It is with blood that humanity has been purified and redeemed, the blood of the Lord. We shall never even try to count the number of children to whom he has given spiritual birth, whom he has borne into new life, into new hope, and into resurrection. We praise him, and we bless him for every window he has opened to us. Every window of his desert is an opening to hope and life.

In his *Desert Windows* Eddie Doherty is seeking the fullness of God and the fullness of life, the fullness of love, and the fullness of giving. Because he was free he completely trusted his humanity. Because he was free he was able to put aside all that he possessed, to be possessed by the Infinite Himself. He honored his commitment to Madonna House Apostolate to multiply life and joy. Madonna House was for him a new vision and a challenge. The adventure took his fancy, and he hung his personal garments on the clothesline of eternity, to give it life. Eddie Doherty loved life passionately. He enjoyed life fully. He suffered from life intensely. Love, joy, and suffering were always with him as an everlasting celebration of freedom. *Desert Windows* opens onto that freedom and onto that celebration.

At last his hay is in. At last his window to paradise has come unstuck and stands wide open. Let us enter in with a hymn of praise, gratitude and joy.

Archbishop Joseph M. Raya
Feast of All Saints, 1976
Madonna House, Combermere

I

THE THREE WINDOWS

Men and women all around me go frequently to the desert, to the poustinia, to the "prayer house" as we call it, taking bread and salt and tea. And thought. And the Book of the words of God. Men and women come from various parts of the world to this insignificant village of Combermere to bury themselves for a day or two in a "retreat."

We began building these poustinias, these prayer houses, a few years ago, intending them for our staff workers. But visitors wanted them too. We kept on building. We are still building. We have bought an island which we will turn into a desert. And eventually it will have its own chapel by which we shall honor Our Lady of the Woods.

All these hermit lodges are made of logs, dead wood, that lie lengthwise in their places in sharp contrast to the living upright trees that tower all around them. A sign of the cross! A wooden web of praise and petition! Log mutters to log the glory of the Lord and tree murmurs to tree unceasingly the prayers of the pilgrim penitents: "God have mercy! God have mercy! God have mercy!"

But none of this should concern me. I have my own poustinia, my private desert—with a built-in oasis—my wasteland wadi, my holy hideout. It is a big room. It is big enough to make me feel at times like a snail inhabiting the cast-off shell of a mammoth turtle. It serves as a bedroom, sitting room, reception room, study, office, den, library, sometimes a dining room, and now and then a private chapel.

The log houses on the island and in other places not too far from Madonna House have windows that let in the sun and air—or the rain or snow, if anyone wants that sort of thing—and the odors of pine trees and wild flowers and bird song and the unceasing chant of the merry Madawaska.

My windows open on an orchard, a parking lot, a stand of tall red pines, a piece of Highway 517, a scramble of buildings, and the bright blue bosom of the river.

But it has other windows that nobody knows about—nobody but myself. These windows, fashioned by a master, oversee the miles and miles of a desert of wilderness and sand—sand poured out of hundreds of thousands of God's own hourglasses.

It is before these windows that I pray and meditate and fast. I may be exempt from fasting because of my age. Yet I fast more often than men much younger and stronger than I am. I fast between meals. And I eat only breakfast, lunch, afternoon tea, dinner, evening tea, and midnight snacks.

No scent of wildflower or pine tree comes into my room; but the delicious whiff of fresh-baked bread, bacon sizzling in a frying pan, and apple pies just taken from the oven, come up from the kitchen through the grates in the floor. The pilgrims on the island love to listen in their contemplative moments to the gossip of the river or to the joyous hymns of the birds. I listen to the laughter and the singing of all the pretty little cooks and dish-washers and dryers and putter-awayers who bless the kitchen underneath my most delightful desert.

Cook to cook sings "Alleluia," and washer to dryer chants praises to Our Lady.

For all I know to the contrary, the prayer houses may be equipped with their own secret windows. It is possible they have more than my room can boast. I have only three. One looks directly into heaven. But it sticks or something. I could never get it open.

The second is a real contemplative's window, but an amateur can get pleasure from it once in awhile, though usually the glass is fogged. (Perhaps I do not always adjust it to the proper angle.) But when the light is right and the glass is clear, how great God is!

The third window has a magic glass that brings far off things close, makes old things new, and even gives life and loveliness to friends who lie asleep in dust and ashes.

Only yesterday I was looking through that magic casement and I saw a little boy. He was in a chapel in a Wisconsin monastery. He was dressed like other boys of his age. White shirt with a high stiff collar. A bow tie. Knee pants, stockings rolled into a sort of garter just above the knees. Scuffed and battered black shoes. He was kneeling before the statue of Our Lady of Sorrows and he was making love—not to the statue but to the Lady it represented.

The statue was tall and slim and beautiful beyond words. Its face was sad, but not too sad. There was something in it that reminded the boy of his mother at home in Chicago; and something that didn't remind him at all of his mother. The boy was happy just to be there alone. There was nothing to do but look at her and at the vigil lights burning before her and at the diamonds Father Prior had fastened on her gown. A woman who said she had been miraculously cured had asked that Our Lady wear the jewels forever on the statue. Sometimes in the candlelight those diamonds winked and blinked like blazing bitter tears.

The boy often thought of the statue and its diamonds and its seven swords and its sweet sad face—even years after he had left the monastery.

And one thing he wondered about—if you must know. That was the Fourth Station of the Cross where Jesus, carrying his heavy burden, suddenly sees his mother.

The ordinary mother would have fought all the Roman soldiers in the neighborhood and all the high priests and Pharisees and Scribes to rescue her son from any danger. Why didn't Mary? Because she knew he was God and could help himself if he wanted to? Maybe! Maybe not! Who knew?

Often, as he came closer and closer to my magic window, he wondered about this problem. I could see that plainly.

What did a woman say to her son when she suddenly discovered he was going to be crucified? What did a man say to his mother? What did their eyes say that their tongues could never utter?

As the boy neared he gradually changed into a pigeon-toed, fat-headed old man with a white mustache. It was hideously like looking into a mirror. I slammed the window shut.

And last night I woke thinking—God forbid—that I had left the television babbling on and on. I turned on a light and got out of bed. The television was—thank you, Lord—serenely silent. But the voice continued speaking. It was coming from outside the first window, the one that always sticks. I turned out the light and listened.

"What does a woman say to her son when she suddenly

discovers he is going to be crucified? She says nothing. What does the man say to his mother. Nothing. These two have no need of words. What do their eyes say that their tongues cannot utter? Listen, and write it down, and never forget it.

"In his mother's eyes the man sees complete, thorough, exquisite understanding of what he is about to do and why he is about to do it. She is the only human being who ever understood him at all; and her understanding—and her complete approval—fills him with a divine joy and with all the strength he needs to continue on to Calvary.

"In her eyes he sees that she has become his partner in the redemption of the world. There is in her a sublime pity for the children of other mothers. It almost matches his own!

"What do their eyes say to each other? They speak of selflessness. They speak of everlasting mercy. They speak of eternal love. They speak of earthly woe and of everlasting joy in heaven."

I didn't write the words. I was too excited. I scrawled only a few notes. I listened again. Someone was singing, someone in ecstasy. Someone who made me think of Mary as she chanted her first Magnificat.

"Beautiful are you, O son of God, my son. Beautiful are you. General of all the armies of the Lord. Beautiful are you in your dirt-stained, sweat-stained, blood-stained robe, in the blood that oozes down your face from the crown of thorns, in the blood that is clotted in your beard and is spattered on your arms—the arms that could gesture to wind and wave and tame them instantly. Beautiful are you in the blood that shines on your bruised and blistered feet—

the feet that tread so lightly on the Sea of Galilee. Beautiful, my Jesus, are you in your uniform of love!"

I thought of that last line for a long, long time. I have thought of it often since then. That uniform, I know, could never fit me. But I think I would rejoice if it were cut down for me—say by his mother—and I were permitted to wear it just for a little time!

I listened for more. But no more was said. I arranged the covers and tried to sleep. Impossible. I was trying to envision Mary standing beneath the great sprawling cross, watching her son die, willing him to die for us, her children. Her wicked children.

She was waiting, I thought, to welcome us—but not until she had said goodbye to her first son and had prepared a parcel which he was to bring to his father, with her love— and the love of all her kin.

The incense of the prayers and the tears of Mary Magdalen and the good thief were in that parcel, I presumed. And the myrrh of remorse. And the shining gold of the new love they had found on Calvary.

I couldn't see Our Lady's face clearly, but I did see two great tears on her cheek. They blazed in the darkness of my desert room like the finest diamonds. And I went to sleep in their splendor.

2

COMBERMERE—TEMPORARY HEAVEN

I have spent nearly a quarter of a century in the midst of saints and saintlings. And this has been the most exciting time of my exciting humpty-dumpty life!

We came to Madonna House, Catherine and I, on May 17, 1947, in a new automobile that looked as big as a locomotive and as expensive as a garage full of Rolls Royces. I had bought it with money borrowed from Bishop Bernard Sheil of Chicago.

We came to a house that was just barely furnished. There was a home-made table, a few home-made chairs, a bed, a stove, and an antiquated pump in the basement that required close to a thousand vigorous up-and-down jerks to supply the upstairs bathroom. There were enough gadgets in the kitchen for the two of us; and I think there was a broom and a mop and half a dozen old-fashioned lamps plus two antique lanterns.

The house was built on a patch of sand. There was sand all around it. There were weeds here and there but no grass, no flowers. And there were tremendous and glorious red pine trees. And there was the majestic blue Madawaska, gently kissing the shores on two sides of us and streaking away from our front steps miles and miles into the unknown!

The house was beautiful and strong. It has been built with great love and with great patience by Nicholas Mackletzoff, a relative by marriage of my Catherine.

Nicholas was a gifted architect, artist, engineer and musician. He intended the house to be a gift someday to a woman he loved—hence he put all his appreciation of beauty into it. The people in and around the tiny village of Combermere, Ontario, Canada, referred to it as "the palace."

Even before we were married, Catherine told me stories about the house and about Combermere and about the people who lived there. The village was, among other things, the most peaceful place in the world and the most beautiful.

I visualized the place as I listened to her and felt glad many a time that I would probably never see it. Who wanted to spend any time in a setting like that? Rest and rest! Quit the big cities and be a rustic? Not me. The big cities were my life. My arteries throbbed to their rhythms. I loved their noises, their slums, their canyons, their crowds, their vices and virtues, their different characters.

I loved Chicago. I loved New York. I loved San Francisco. I loved New Orleans. I loved London and Paris and Jerusalem and Rome and Havana and Stockholm and Copenhagen and many other great cities. I loved travelling—always at the expense of some magazine or newspaper. I loved spending money and somehow I managed to spend a lot of it—and make a lot of it.

The Russian woman changed me, subtly, slowly, in her own delicious way. We hadn't been married long before I found myself—to my utter disbelief and horror—promising to live in "holy poverty" with her. I was the "battleship" in the editorial room of the Chicago Sun. I had a top salary. I was given the best assignments. Everything was going my way. Yet, one day in August 1945, I decided to visit Combermere. Surely, I told myself I could stand the country for two weeks. I might even make Catherine think I liked it. (That would please her.)

So I entered the house and surveyed its cosy loveliness. Then I sat at the home-made table in the "living room" downstairs, and I looked at the Madawaska sparkling in the young May sun. And I said aloud—again to my disbelief and horror—"I am going to buy this house."

I bought it. It didn't occur to me that I had a promise of poverty. If it occurred to Catherine, she didn't mention it. I had sold a book and Catherine hadn't had time to give all the royalties to her friends, the poor. So the house was mine—ours.

August 15, 1945 was Catherine's birthday and V-J Day, the end of the Second World War. Bishop William Smith, newly consecrated for the See of Pembroke, visited Madonna House for the first time on that day. He asked Catherine to start "some sort of catholic action" for his people who, he said, were "among the poorest of the poor."

"I will do what I can," Catherine said, "*when* I can. Right now we cannot leave Chicago. I am the director-general of Friendship House with headquarters in Chicago. And Eddie, as you know, is working on a newspaper in that city. But if the Lord wants me here he will arrange things so that we can come and help you. Now that we own the house . . ."

Something in her voice alarmed me. Now that we owned the house. I was crazy! Why did I buy a house? So I could spend two weeks in it every year? Or for some reason I didn't know and never could understand?

I had learned to be uneasy whenever Catherine began to

talk business with a bishop. Bishops had ways of changing a man's life. I could testify to that. I was even more uneasy listening to her say, "Now that we own the house."

A year later the Chicago Sun found itself in such a financial mud-hole that it had to get rid of three hundred or more of its high-salaried men. About the same time Catherine came to the agonizing belief that she should resign as director-general of Friendship House and go to Canada to help "the poorest of the poor."

It wasn't at all like St. Paul's vision of being called to Macedonia; but it amounted to the same thing.

The Sun gave me something over $5,000 in severance pay. I thought that would keep us in comfort until I could find another job. Why shouldn't it? We lived in poverty in a one-room flat in East Walton Place. And the rent was only one dollar a day. Five thousand was enough to keep us for a year! I didn't realize until later that it wouldn't last a month with the poor people of Chicago's Friendship House.

The day came when we had nothing but the furniture in the flat, the clothes we wore, and the house in Combermere.

We didn't have money enough for bus fare. So we bought that big automobile with the Bishop's money and an extra thousand dollars loaned us by my friend, Father John Ireland Gallery. We loaded the car with books, a reproduction of the picture of Our Lady of Guadalupe, and all the cooking utensils and dishes we had.

We arrived sometime in the afternoon and found a few dozen young apple trees which Catherine had ordered by mail. They were lying in the sand back of the house. One of our neighbors, Wilfrid Bouchard, planted them all while I watched. He was a wizard with shovel and spade. He offered to teach me the art but somehow I never had time to learn it.

I remember the bullfrogs that kept me awake most of the evening and the birds that woke me early in the morning. I remember the first time I dug a ditch in which to plant rhubarb and almost broke my back. I remember the days when I was trying to write enough books to keep us alive and everybody in the countryside came to interrupt me— "Where's the Baroness? Where's Catherine? Where's the B? Where's the missus? My wife is going to have a baby, where's your wife?"

We were alone, just the two of us. No money coming, no money in the house, tradesmen making jokes about our credit being good and how much they liked our house.

Our credit was good—undoubtedly because of the magnificent appearance of our car; the fact that Catherine had been a "countess or something," and the belief that I was some kind of crazy millionaire. So we survived.

Eventually, one of the original Friendship House staff workers came to live with us. People began to send money and clothes and furniture and even food. Neighbors brought us buckets of wild strawberries or the hindquarters of a deer. God was good to us. So were people.

Strangely enough, I never tired of the new life forced upon me. I agreed with Catherine that Canada was one of the most beautiful countries in the world and that our section was lovelier than any other. I loved the people. I loved some of their expressions: "The poor lad didn't have on enough clothes to cover a gooseberry"—"the way she screamed you'd think she was giving birth to a porcupine"—"he's a good man but you dasn't contrary him."

I loved their hospitality. I loved their honesty and their constant offer to help in any way they could. I loved the river and the dirt roads and the tall strong-scented pines and the little bits of feldspar that greeted me with such vivid flashes of color when the sun shone on them. I loved the millions of pine cones scattered over all the earth and the wildflowers and the meadows and the happy hillsides and the music of wind in the woods.

I realized that God had taken me out of Chicago only to place me in a paradise. I realized that I no longer loved a man-made city; that I was infatuated by a "brand new" God-made world. I realized also that this particular world, attractive and vital as it was, was also a desert—my own particular desert.

I was a stranger here. I would always be a stranger. I was practically a hermit. A hermit without a permit; but a hermit just the same. Me, the gabby gadabout, the newspaperman who always had to be where the shooting was. I had become a hermit! And, what was sillier still, I loved it! I was free at last. I was at peace. I had nothing whatever to do except to love God and all his creatures and to trust in him for everything I needed.

I felt this most keenly after my trip to the Pembroke General Hospital in 1948. I was driven there late at night on the 29th of February with the Northern Lights dancing gloriously in the frosty skies and all the bright stars winking. Our pastor, God love him, Father Pat Dwyer gave me the last rites of the church before I got into the taxi and he thrust $15 into my hands. I was supposed to have a coronary thrombosis. But the doctor said it was a mere infarction and that my heart was good for thirty years at least. I tried to bargain with him for forty years, thirty-five, thirty-four. He was adamant. No more than thirty. Why should any man want more?

I came home in a few days but I was weak for many months—too weak to dig in the garden, to shovel snow, to help Catherine in any way. There were days when I couldn't even lift a newspaper! So I stayed outdoors lying on one of those store-bought city-slicker things and watched the world march through the seasons.

It was there, I think, that I knew God wanted me to spend the rest of my life in the Madonna House Apostolate. It was there that I became convinced that I should write love letters to God and print them every month in *Restoration,* our family paper.

It was there I began to watch heaven working on the young men and women who had come to see *"what* Madonna House was all about." This was much more fascinating than watching Wilfrid Bouchard with his magic shovel. People were transformed every day. They submitted to the work in awe but with some reluctance at first. After a while they cooperated eagerly. They accepted the love they found in Madonna House. They decked themselves in it. They began to love.

Love transfigured them, made their eyes shine, made them sing, made them laugh, made them work as though they were being paid an ounce of gold for every hour. Nobody was ever paid for anything in Madonna House. Nobody ever worked harder anywhere in the world than the staff workers of Madonna House. They worked for the sheer love of God and the love of each other. Catherine kept saying, "Love one another—love one another—love one another."

For thirty years I have listened to Catherine talking to young people. For thirty years I have heard the same question asked, sometimes over and over and over. For thirty years I have listened to Catherine's answers. And somehow, believe it or not, I have never been bored!

It was there I watched the first staff workers marching through the seasons of God. No newspaper story I have ever covered held such wonder, such suspense, such triumph.

It was there I began to see that my job was to keep out of Catherine's way—not to interfere with her management of the house and the apostolate. All I had to do was to stay in my hermitage. God and Our Lady would help her more than I could. I could trust them. I should trust them. I did trust them. So what did I have to worry about?

I had only one window in my desert then—the one that showed me all my yesterdays. I didn't use it much. I didn't like the view.

Without any aid from me, Madonna House grew and grew and grew. People came from the ends of the earth— some to stay for awhile, some to give it their lives. Donations multiplied. We began to build even when we had no money to build with. We built something like a whole village. We kept building because everything we built became too small too soon. More and more people came. Father John T. Callahan came to preach a retreat and stayed to become our first chaplain and later on the director-general of the priests. Now we have thirteen priests in the apostolate—and more than thirty associate priests.

Priests! At first there was only Father Pat and often his stomach was so bad he couldn't say mass. We had no chaplain, no spiritual director until Father Callahan arrived. Almost immediately Madonna House began to flower. Bishops came from east and west, north and south, to ask for help.

We began to establish Madonna Houses in many parts of the world.

It was a tremendous day for us when, in 1941, Father Gallery came from Chicago and said a mass in our living room—which was also our library and our main dining room and our assembly hall. His was the first mass said in the house. A year or so after Father Callahan came, we built a chapel. We had no money but we built the chapel. And soon there will be a chapel on the island we've acquired.

Originally we had five acres and the house. Now there are over 1,500 acres, and we have more houses and dormitories in Combermere and a dozen other parts of the world than any hermit ever dreamed of having.

My hermitage grew also. And I have three windows now. Besides the one looking on my yesterdays, one looks on Galilee and Judea and those parts of Egypt where the refugee son of God fled for safety. My other window looks on heaven. I can't open it. I can't see out of it. But sometimes I hear the voice of someone standing just outside it.

Rejoice with us. I am not the only hermit here. For

twenty-five years I have lived in a desert. For twenty-five years I have lived in a temporary heaven. Rejoice with us. All of us. We all live in a temporary heaven. Someday the Lord will transfer us to his permanent heaven. See you there. Rejoice. Rejoice. Rejoice.

3

YOUNG MAN, ARISE!

Of the three windows of my private desert, the first one is my favorite. Its magic brings far things close and gives life to long dead incidents and long lost friends and loved ones.

Through this window yesterday I saw a huddle of stone houses high on a sunlit hill—the village of Naim, not far from fragrant Nazareth, not far from Magdala. A long string of goats was winding up one twisting narrow path, painting a tar-black streak through the dust that rose and glittered in the sunshine. A long string of men and women in white robes was trickling slowly down another path, lamenting loudly the death of a young man, the only son of his mother, who was a widow.

And there, at the place where the two paths said "hail" and "farewell" to each other, stood my Lord Jesus. He was looking at the dead man's mother; and his face was beautiful with compassion and with love.

I think he has a special love for widows, not only because his mother was one of them, but because a widow is much more a symbol and a source of love than is a bride. She has known the wonder and the glory and the delight and the pain of her husband's love. Now that all this is gone, she realizes how blessed she was and how grateful she should be for this gift of God. Her man is dead. But love is eternal and inexhaustible. It still strengthens her. It still enriches her. She has love to lavish on everyone around her. And she

gives it freely to all who suffer pain or grief or need of any
kind.

A bride brings her husband a dowry of love; a widow
inherits the major part of his heart's estate.

"When the Lord saw her," St. Luke wrote, "his heart
went out to her and he said, 'Weep no more.' With that he
stepped forward and laid his hand on the bier; and the
bearers halted. Then he spoke: 'Young man, rise up.' The
dead man rose up and began to talk, and Jesus gave him
back to his mother."

What was it like, to wake from the dead and look into the
eyes of the son of God? What is it like to wake from the
dead and know you are alive?

Years ago in a hospital I sat up in bed conscious of being,
but not sure whether I lived in this world or the next.

Newspaper men often quote the opening of a cub
reporter's story, "John Jones was at death's door, but the
doctor pulled him through." I remembered that line and
wondered about it. I had had a serious operation. Had the
doctor pushed me in or out of death's half-open door?

I was looking through a window, but there was nothing to
see. Everything was black. Deep black. Then a cloud
moved, and I saw the yellow moon—the most beautiful
thing I ever saw.

I went happily to sleep and woke to look into the eye of a
fresh-fried egg. Now for many years I had hated, shunned,
refused, scorned, rejected, avoided, and escaped all eggs,
however cooked. But this one captured me at sight. I
stabbed its eye with an eager fork and rejoiced at the flood
of golden tears it offered. It was so good to be alive!

It still is. I can hardly wait—some mornings—for my
breakfast egg.

I would rather go through the eye of an egg than be a millionaire.

A hush spread through the crowd that surrounded Jesus; and I could hear a woman weeping both in happiness and in sorrow. I could not see her, but I imagined she was holding her son in love and joy and lamenting passionately that her husband was not there to share this moment with her. Then the dust rose everywhere up to the line of baa-ing goats—thus pulling my window shades not down but up, to end the spectacle.

What became of the dead man, I wondered? Did he live happily ever after? Did everybody think him a freak? Did he become a follower of Jesus? What did the Lord have in mind for him when he gave him back to his mother? And why, incidentally, did he give life to Lazarus and the pretty little daughter of Jairus? What happened to those two?

I know what happened to me.

I was dead once. As dead as Lazarus. And stinking in the tomb of the flesh. The Lord bade me come forth. Someone rolled the stone. And I went into the fresh air and poured out all the corruption of my sepulchral life in a confessional in St. Francis of Assisi Church in the city of New York. Even the angels envied the happiness I felt then. I did not see the face of Jesus. I didn't know enough to look for it in the faces of every man. What I did know was that Jesus had wept for me too even as he had for Lazarus. It was hard to believe. But I knew that it was so.

I lay a long time thinking. There was nothing else to do. One window was dusted over. The contemplatives' window was fogged. And the window that stares all day and all night at heaven still refused to open.

The young man of Naim was a symbol of the Church, I thought. The Church was dead and on its way to oblivion when Christ approached the crossroads. He brought it back and gave it to his own mother, our beautiful Virgin Mary.

Could it have been her whom I heard, the woman who wept for sorrow and for joy, holding her Church in her arms? There is so much goodness and happiness and holiness and love in that Church! There is so much pain in it, so much woe, so much ignorance, so much scandal, and so very much rebellion. Jesus might speak of it as he spoke of the little girl. "She is not dead but sleeping." He might bring her back to life and he might say to her mother, "Give her something to eat."

Mary, please give your Church *something* to eat!

4

THE FACES OF JESUS

The face of Jesus stares up at me from a dirty sidewalk on West Madison Street, Chicago.

It has waited there a long time trying to attract my attention so that I might help to attract the attention of the world. Many rains have not washed that face away, nor cleansed the blood from its lips. Snows have covered it, but only temporarily. Passing cars have spattered it with mud and filth. Sanitation trucks have often spilled their garbage on it. Dogs have profaned it. Drunks have fallen on it and cursed it. Drunks have spewed their vomit on it. But it lies there still, patient as the day it fell, waiting for me. For me or for you?

West Madison Street! Newspapermen call it "the street of lost and forgotten men . . . the boulevard of beggars and bums . . . the highway of the wino and the weary Willie . . . the path to the lockup and the morgue."

Through the secret windows of my desert—this room above the kitchen of Madonna House—I have seen the face of Jesus often. It is strong and beautiful and royal and compassionate. But it does not stir me too much—for it is a painting, done in a hurry by my imagination. The face on the sidewalk—which my imagination also painted—thrills me so much that I must write about it. Why?

Someone once said I might find the face of Jesus in the people all around me. I have looked closely many times. But I have yet to find "him whom my soul loveth."

A few nights ago I sought him in a prayer meeting held in one of the new log cabins on the island—our poustinia. The bishop, the priests, the nuns, and the lay people—I searched the countenance of each one. He was not there. They were looking for him too. Or perhaps they were looking at him!

I retreated to my desert windows, thinking I know not what—maybe that I would see him come toward me, "leaping upon the mountains, skipping upon the hills . . . showing himself through the lattice." But as usual one window stuck. One—that favored by the contemplatives—was covered by frost, exquisitely designed with lilies and tulips and irises and asphodels and shamrocks. But no good to me. Only one was in working order. This is the window that looks upon the sand and the cactus and the wastelands and the gardens of my past. I opened it wide.

Someone, a familiar figure, was gazing at a picture in a store window. Somewhere in Manhattan. He was so enchanted by what he saw that he could not move his flat pigeon-toed feet. I went behind him, looked over one of his dandruff-sprinkled shoulders, and beheld the beauty that had stopped and stunned him, a picture of the Little Infant of Prague. A painting, not a statue.

"Now the artist," I said to the man, merging with him. "C. Bosseron Chambers. He must have a phone. Let's talk to him."

We talked to him. He told us a story about a girl who lived in the Bronx and worked in downtown Manhattan as a private secretary to a man famous both in Washington, D.C. and on Wall Street. One night in her home she was helping her mother with the dishes—that's the sort of girl she was—when she felt sharp pains in her bosom.

She rushed to the bathroom mirror and saw a mysterious and awesome thing, a crucifix that had been etched into the flesh between her breasts. An exquisite Christ was depicted there. His head hanging to the left. No. To the right. It moved now and then! It moved!

Eventually, of course, she went to a convent in up-state New York. The first day there she fell and broke a hip. For years she lay in bed, the happiest woman in the world. And a crucifix, as beautiful and as mysterious as the one above her heart, appeared on the wall of her cell.

This was, naturally, a great distraction for all the other nuns so the mother superior tried to erase it. Plaster couldn't hide it. Acids couldn't eat away any part of it. Cement fell off it. It shone through paint, through varnish, through shellac—even through soap and water. It disappeared only when the sister died.

"Once," Mr. Chambers told us, "I was in a fever to paint a real image of Christ. I picked many models. I picked them carefully. I worked with them tirelessly for weeks. I destroyed every picture. I fired every model. I rushed away to Europe to avoid a nervous breakdown and to see what models I might find in France, in Italy, in Greece, in the Holy Land. I came home in something like despair. But I couldn't give up.

"I decided to paint without a model. I worked all day and all night and all the next day. I wasn't satisfied. Then I had a happy idea. Why not show the picture to the nun with the cross? I left it with her overnight. In the morning, when I was allowed to see her, she said, 'It's good. The beard should be a trifle brighter. But don't touch it. Don't do any more to it.' "

We looked at the picture, the pigeon-toed writer and I. We liked it. It was beautiful. It was strong. It was compassionate. But we forgot it when we left the studio.

I have never printed the story of this extraordinary nun who may be canonized some day. The cardinal archbishop asked me not to. It would bring more tourists to the convent than the World's Fair brought to New York—and the nuns wouldn't have time to meditate or pray or do anything but speculate.

"I sought him whom my soul loveth, but I found him not."

I was about to shut the window when I happened to see West Madison Street—a thousand miles distant from the artist's studio—and noticed an old friend kneeling on the sidewalk, evidently looking for something he had lost. He had his thick spectacles in his hand. He was sweeping the walk with his eyelashes. And he was assuring the world that he was the ill-begotten son of a sheep-killing mongrel yellow dog.

"Whatcha lose?" I asked him.

"My St. Anthony medal, damn it," he said.

"I didn't know you were a catholic, Blinky," I said.

"I ain't," he assured me. "But that medal saved my life at least twice. It's my lucky piece. I always keep it in my pocket. Every little while I run my fingers over it. Horse shoes? Four leaf clovers? The left hind leg of a rabbit killed in a graveyard? Superstitions! But that medal . . . if that's gone my luck is gone. Forever."

"St. Anthony," I told him, "is the finder of lost things.
Ask him to look for it. You can't go wrong."

"To hell with that," Blinky exploded. "Let's get a drink.
I got something on my mind and I gotta get rid of it."

I bought the drink. Blinky always left his money in his
other pants. He sat there blinking at me, sipping his beer as
though it were a poison—and good enough for him.

"I was on my way to the Hearst building," he said,
"when this moocher came at me. At first I thought he was a
drunk. He acted like a drunk. He said he was hungry and
wanted some money. He said he hadn't eaten in three days.
He lurched toward me like a drunk and I tried to get out of
his way. 'Beat it, bum,' I said. 'If you wanta eat, go get
yourself a job.'

" 'But mister, there ain't no jobs,' he said, and he put a
dirty hand on my shoulder. With that I ups to his jaw and
he falls to the cement. And there's blood trickling out of his
mouth.

"I was sorry I hit him. I bent over him. He wasn't drunk.
He did look hungry. Skin and bones. I thought he was
dead. I called a cop and the paddy wagon took him away.
When I got to the office I reached into my pocket for the
medal. It was gone. St. Anthony had deserted me. He had
lammed. I don't blame him. I wish I could lam too. I never
hit a bum before. And out of all the bums in Chicago I had
to hit one who was starving! My mother would say I hit
Christ. Maybe I did. I'll never have any more luck so long
as I live."

That was fifty odd years ago, and in those days I kept my
religion far away from my larynx—and, I guess, far away
from my heart too. I helped him hunt for the medal before I

left him. And I didn't see him until thirty years later. Then quite by accident I discovered that he and his wife were living in a poorly furnished room near the Cathedral. His wife was sick and he had no money. No doctor had come to see her. He was out of a job. He couldn't pay the rent. He couldn't buy even a pack of cigarettes.

"St. Anthony never forgets and never forgives," he said. "God forgives, but he doesn't forget."

I tried a wisecrack. "God is the supreme eraser. Does any eraser remember what it has rubbed out? God is a beggar. I've walked away from him many times. Maybe I never hit him but I have said again and again, 'Beat it, bum! Scram!' But he came back still begging a word from me, a prayer, a 'thank you,' a little show of love. I couldn't get rid of him. One day he hit me hard and I crawled on my hands and knees, begging a kind word from him."

Before I closed the window, I looked at West Madison Street again. The bum lying on the sidewalk was Blinky. Then, gradually, the face changed. And I saw "him whom my soul had sought." Jesus, in rags, trying to get up.

There was the same beauty in him I had seen in Chambers' painting—and in many other pictures. There was the same masculinity and compassion. But this face had more. It had a royal dignity. It had a pity that was almost haunting. It had a sense of truth and justice. And it had a divine anger, and a fearful wrath.

5

UNFORGETTABLE DAYS

The train speeds westward to new and old locations, to new and old friends, to new adventures, to new stories, and perhaps to a new assortment of the Lord's own jewelry, the petrified wood of Arizona.

And my thoughts drift, as they will, back to Combermere and to Chicago, back to the wonderful year of 1970. I have no idea what the future will bring me; but I am sure it will never be more generous than the past. Somebody on the train (was it only myself?) asked me awhile ago what was the happiest day of the last year.

I thought of anniversaries. The twenty-seventh return of my last wedding day. The first anniversary of my ordination to the priesthood when I became a Nazarene. The eightieth anniversary of my birthday. (That was certainly a wonderful day.) Only once in a lifetime does any man have an eightieth birthday! My second Christmas as a priest—my second opportunity to celebrate the divine liturgy three times in one day.

I think of many other days and thanked the Lord again and again for them. But two days—and I couldn't pin a date on either one of them—shone on me like brilliant stars—two ordinary days.

One of these beautiful and blessed occasions occurred sometime in November. I am sure of that because I have a letter to prove it.

It must have snowed during the night for I remember the

dawn crept into my room in beautiful white mukluks; and I greeted her with a joyous lyric, though I was half asleep.

> "Shall I arise at once and face
>   The arrows of the day?
> Or lie awhile in God's sweet grace,
>   And thank him that I may?"

Somebody answered me. Somebody who had just come in to wake me. My friend, Father Emile Briere.

"What are you mumbling about?" he demanded.

"What time is it?" I answered. I always answer people in that way.

"Time for mass," he said.

"Miraculous," I told him. I got up wondering what had made me so elated. Something I had eaten or drunk? No. My nurses still tell me, "If you like it, spit it out!" It must have been something I read. Of course! It was a paragraph or two written by Joan Bryant, one of our staff workers. Joan is an artist. She paints with oils as well as with words. She paints with beauty. I kept her letter. Let me show you what I mean.

"The brilliant greens have turned into soft grays, pale yellows, and warm rusts. The bushy trees are now like cobwebs or lace against the pale gray skies. The sun's brilliant light no longer makes strong orange light on the old building" (the railway station at Barry's Bay, which she was then painting into an outstanding canvas) "and there is almost no light after 2:30." (What things an artist notices!) I certainly couldn't finish the painting from memory, so carefully I exchanged the early autumn colors for late fall and hoped it wouldn't snow before noon.

"Lord, what a marvelous artist you are! As I clumsily grope to try to translate your colors and forms into some kind of order I begin to try to appreciate the beauty and order of your world. Where will I ever find the patience or the brush that will be able to paint the branches of a tree that looks like a lace fan? How can one even begin to capture the beauty of a sky that is, in one hour, brilliant azure . . . and the next moment pale blue, with gray, pink, and white clouds?"

That was, undoubtedly, the reason for my exaltation. The mood continued through the mass—and indeed through all the rest of the day. When I received the host at communion I caressed it as though it were indeed a lamb . . . "This is the lamb of God. . . ." I kissed it and put it into my mouth. And I felt as though I were a shepherd and there were green pastures all around me and still waters and new-born lambs with their mothers. And when I drank from the chalice I felt that a warm rain was falling everywhere about me, waking a million wildflowers, thrilling a grove full of thirsty birds so that they sang a hymn to the Lord, freshening and cleansing the whole wide world all around me, and making it fragrant.

That was a day to remember always. And so was the day late in December when I celebrated the divine liturgy, the Eastern-rite mass in the home of my sisters Kathleen and Eileen and my brother Tom in Chicago. Tom was late in coming home from work that day. And I saved communion for him.

It lay in front of me a long long while, the glorified body

of Christ—looking like an ordinary piece of bread—on a shining white napkin. I sat on a chair in front of it keeping my green alb and my stole on me, the symbols of my priesthood, and taking a rosary into my hands. My sisters busied themselves in the kitchen while I sat alone with Christ the Lord, "him whom my soul loveth."

This was such a rare privilege I didn't know what to do. So I didn't do anything—except say one rosary after the other. And at times I thought we were saying it together!

There was Christ himself before me. There was I, another Christ, another Nazarene. What a miracle! I had been ordained in my 79th year. I had never studied theology or philosophy. I had never been to high school or to college. I had been married three times and was still a married man. Rome had twice refused my petition to be made a priest. And then, after three months of study in the Holy Land, a Melkite bishop put his holy hands on me. And I became another Christ! This in, of all places in the world, a convent chapel in Nazareth of Galilee. What should I say now to him? He knew all that was in my heart, all my intentions, all my wishes for Madonna House, and for all my relatives and friends, and for all the so-called "riff-raff" of the world, the winos, the whiners, the naggers, the harlots, the ignorant, the savage, the murderous, the unskilled, the unwanted, the deserted, the prisoners—prisoners of war and prisoners of peace—the shameful, the disgraced, the exploited, the despairing, the criminals of the world.

There was no need for talk between us. But somehow he reminded me of the story of the poor old man who went into a church every day and just sat in a pew. He didn't pray. He didn't read any spiritual books. As he said himself he "just sat and looked at God and let God look at him." For the first time I realized the riches of the joy that poor man owned.

At times, of course, I looked at him through my desert windows. It seems these are portable. It seems also that I packed them somehow with my other things, though I have no recollection of this. I found them with me—the window that looks on heaven—still frosted on the outside, still sticking—the one that looks on Galilee and Judea, and the one that looks on all the hills and valleys and deserts and swamps and oases of my life.

And I saw the Son of Man sitting on the snowy top of a mountain, talking to his father. And I saw him lying on the white sands and the desert after he had fasted forty days and forty nights. And I saw him lying on a great patch of snow on the island across from Madonna House in Combermere—the circular patch where the new chapel will be built this spring and summer. Hermit Island, I call it.

If I thought of any one thing in particular during all this unexpected and delicious time, it was "how to become a saint." After my ordination one of my grandsons wrote me, "First step, the priesthood, second step, sanctity." Sanctity! I must become a saint! But how? By wearing a hair shirt? That is good for some people. Not for me. By scourging myself? Oh no! Anybody but me! By fasting? My doctors and nurses won't let me. By rubbing cigarette stubs in my food or using nauseating ingredients? Unthinkable! Who can spoil any food while so many millions of people starve?

Jesus fasted, but only for those forty days and nights. We never heard that he spoiled his food, wore hair shirts, whipped himself or did anything extraordinary in the way of atonement. We do know that he accepted joyfully whatever indignity, humiliation, rejection, or suffering his father willed him to suffer. We know also that he died the death his father wanted him to die. So it occurred to me to follow him in this—to accept, with such love and gratitude as I can all the penances the most high wishes me to suffer for his sake.

My brother was an hour or more late. But I was almost sorry to see him. He had come too soon, much too soon.

The train stops only at important stations. Time stops at important stations too. And there are two important stops this month, Candlemas Day, February 2, and St. Valentine's Day, February 14.

On February 2, this year, Catherine and I will celebrate our twentieth year as slaves of Jesus in Mary. We gave him everything we were, body and soul, and everything we had, including Madonna House and everything in it, and all the good things we had put into the storehouse of heaven. We gave ourselves forever to Jesus Christ through the hands of his holy mother. And she—and he—have taken excellent care of us ever since.

Jesus, son of Mary; Jesus, son of God—we let him do all our worrying, all our planning. Therefore, we have nothing to worry about.

This St. Valentine's Day will mark the thirtieth anniversary of my first "lover's quarrel" with my wife, Catherine. On February 14, in 1938, she opened her Friendship House in Harlem, New York. I didn't meet her until some time in the autumn of 1940. On February 14th, 1941, I sent her a cartload of violets. Well, maybe not a cartload. Maybe just a wheelbarrow load. (Well, maybe not that much either.) Still it was a big bunch I sent her by Western Union messenger. (And it gets bigger every year).

She didn't mention the violets when I next saw her. In fact she didn't mention anything. She sort of "snooted" me. Maybe violets gave her hay fever, I thought—but who cares what I thought? Eventually she explained she felt hurt because I had ignored her anniversary.

"But I sent you a scuttle full of violets," I protested.

"You sent me a scuttle full of nothing," she said.

She was so positive that she began to ask questions of the people in her apartment building. And one young girl explained. "But you see, Baroness, you weren't home. And there were the violets just outside your door. And I was going to a dance. And they were just what I needed. And so, and so . . . ."

"And so," Catherine said, seizing the culprit in her arms and kissing her, "and so you wore them to the ball! God bless you!"

If I had thought of it at the time, looking at Jesus resting on his gleaming white linen throne, I might have asked him to be my valentine. But I would not have volunteered to be his.

Not yet! I'm far from ready to be the sort of valentine he'd like. What kind would he like me to be? I don't know; but his mother knows. And she'll help me to be what I must be. Why should I worry?

6

WINDOWS ONTO CANYON DIABLO

Showers and showers of angels poured into my room one day, here in the desert of Arizona, singing "Hail Mary, full of grace." I didn't see them with my eyes nor hear them with my ears. Only the sudden wild happiness that flooded my heart told me unmistakably, they were there. I reached for my rosary. The rosary is a harp with 60 strings; and the Lord never tires of listening to the music it sends up. I harked while the angels sang.

Few mornings begin like that. Usually I don't even think about angels when I awake, nor do I always reach out to touch the royal harp. But usually I have the taste of heaven on my lips. Not actually. Just the memory of a taste; the memory of the last divine liturgy, yesterday's mass sung in the Melkite-rite.

Yesterday I sang this mass like one crying out in the wilderness, "Make straight the ways of the Lord." It was at Two Guns, Arizona, at Dave Branch's trading post which takes its name from a deep ravine nearby, Canyon Diablo, the devil's canyon. The altar was a long table set up in a room, an extension of the post which is yet to be finished. There were not enough chairs for the congregation, so a plank was placed over two small "horses." On this the women and children sat. Some of the men stood all through the ceremony.

Peace and good will to men in Two Guns! Holy, holy, holy, Devil's Canyon!

The warmth and brilliance of the sun came in through a window behind me. Through another window I could see the desert stretching immeasurable miles to the horizon. A thousand shades of gold speeding through the sunlight to the comfort and ease of its lazy violet mountain couch, and the clean white pillows that had been tossed on the bottom of the lady-blue sky.

While the staff workers of our Madonna House Apostolate were getting the altar ready for me, I went outside and watched an Indian couple carry a week's supply from the store and drive away in a new red truck. I watched for many minutes, enjoying the wind and the sun and hoping to see more life around me. It was a lonesome place, an isolated region. The only life that answered my call was a long, long freight train singing a song of bargains as it hurried to the East.

I remembered I had my portable windows with me, the magic panes that open on so many places. So I looked at the mystical desert back home in Combermere. Four neat, stout well-built, snow-covered log houses hiding in the trees on Hermit Island—across the stream from Madonna House. Four pumps adorned with shining icicles. Four heaps of firewood, each buried deep in the snow and waiting the broom and the axe. Four wavering columns of gray smoke rising like prayer to the skies. And a great wide circular clearing across the road where the chapel will be built this spring. I looked at the tall trees that almost surround the place. They stood straight, arms linked, solid against the wind continually blessing themselves with all their twigs and branches.

A desert of prayer and meditation and contemplation. A desert of penance and of atonement for sins. A desert occupied now by only four women. A desert pregnant with chapel.

And here at Two Guns a desert of golden shrubs and stones and gopher holes and sun, and people waiting for a priest to sing mass where no mass had ever been sung or said before! I went in and sang the mass and feasted on the "gifts" that were left over after communion. Divine leftovers! The taste of heaven!

What it is to be a priest!

Shortly before mass began, one of the girls in the house came in with a heavy bell in her hand. "Can I ring it, Father?" she asked. I nodded my silly head, thinking she was going to summon other people. But she didn't do that. She rang it at the consecration; and it had the sweetest sound ever heard from a bell. Later I learned it had come from a chapel in Mexico more than a hundred and fifty years ago; and the likeness of the Blessed Virgin was embossed upon it. Our Lady turns up when one least expects her. And always she brings joy. "Hail Mary, full of grace!"

Sometime after the mass—and the dinner cooked by Mrs. Branch—I again opened the window that brings back people and places I have known, and things—sinful and not sinful—I have done. And immediately I saw another kind of wilderness, another kind of world.

I was looking at Palm Desert, California, and reliving my visit there with my brother Bill and his wife Marge, the loveliest of all the O'Malleys.

We motored there from Bill's house in Los Alamitos, a distance of a hundred miles or so—"just down the road a piece"—so that I might again see Frances Rich, the great friend of our Apostolate, the world-famous sculptor who gave us the statue of Our Lady of Combermere.

She had recently completed a heroic statue of St. Francis of Assisi for a friend and then made one for herself, which she put outside her studio; and I was impatient to have a look at it. It stands high on a rocky mound and blesses all the Coachella Valley and all the mountains round about the valley—violet lazy mountains, like those in Arizona, sleeping at the foot of the sky.

We drove out of Palm Desert, fourteen miles up a narrow road, up and around, up and around, up, up, and around, and around, and finally we came to the Shumway road and the studio we sought. A desert and a garden! Cactus everywhere, beauty everywhere. Beauty outside the studio and many kinds of beauty inside.

We sat a long time on the front porch looking down three or four thousand feet (our gaze slanting across a rock-garden only God could have made) into the lush green valley and the hazy mountains; looking up, now and then, to the glory of St. Francis and the little bird that clung to his finger. We talked of the desert. We talked of art. We talked of Our Lady of Combermere. We talked of Irene Rich, Frances' mother, who was the most regal and beautiful of all the movie stars of her day. We talked of holiness and joy and love—love of neighbor and love of God.

Somehow I felt at home in that atmosphere. Actually, I felt there was not much difference between this beautiful and gracious genius and the staff workers of Madonna House. Frances Rich is not a catholic, but I know catholics who are not nearly so devoted to the spreading of Christ's word. I know many who do not live the gospel with their lives as she does.

I compared her mentally with Catherine and the other contemplatives in our snow-covered cabins on Hermit Island.

These women praise God by their prayers, by their labors, by the things they make with their hands, and the articles they write. Frances Rich praises him by making statues of his mother or the infant Jesus, and of his saints. And she puts so much holiness into them that a man is overwhelmed—and forced to wonder. How could she give such glorious life to clay, wax or stone? Where does she find these powerful emotions? Where else but in herself? No woman gives what she doesn't have. You see a saint, you see the sculptor.

Frances showed us a little clay figure of St. Mary Magdalen—one of my favorites in all heaven. The remorse and anguish I saw there made me almost fall on my knees!

Here in her desert, working alone, working in peace and love, working continuously, happily, and with great skill, Frances is a contemplative divinely inspired.

Thousands have come to Madonna House, Combermere, to see her great bronze statue of Our Lady, to pray and meditate there, to weep as the Magdalen weeps, to ask favors, to beg for help, in thanks for many blessings. Pilgrims flock to her other statues wheresoever they may be. Pilgrims will visit her statues through all the years to come—so long as they exist. Maybe her works, her prayers, will live forever, bringing souls to God.

Frances Rich's studio in Palm Desert is actually a shrine.

A cold wind came around the corner of the trading post at Canyon Diablo and chilled the back of my neck. I shut the magic window and went inside—to bless a statue of the Virgin, for which Dave Branch has a great love. I also blessed the bell that bore Our Lady's image.

Then I knew why I felt so good in the mountain studio, and why I felt so at ease in the trading post with the devil's name above its door.

Our Lady! She is our mother. Frances'. Dave's. Mine. And the Madonna House staff workers' who came with me. Through her we are all related. Blood kin. Almost, you might say, "kissing cousins."

Hail Mary, full of grace!

Mary takes a delight in introducing her beloved children to one another. There is always an agape when we assemble in her name, a banquet of love and understanding, a sharing of all the riches of high heaven.

And such happiness overtakes us on these occasions that we fill the desert world with celestial fragrance and make it bloom like a new Eden.

Through Our Lady, our mother, we can give everybody on earth the taste of heaven!

Manna in the desert? All the manna you can hold!

And—it seems—only in the desert!

7

A DREAM

Dear Everybody that I love. This is a letter of thanks and good wishes. I am home from the hospital. I am at the Casa in Arizona. I weigh 30 pounds less than when I went in. I am still weak and will probably have to stay here beyond Easter. Thanks for all your letters, all your get-well cards, all the little things you bought me or sent me, and especially for your prayers.

Let me tell you about a dream I had this morning, April 1, my last day at the hospital. I seemed to find myself just inside the doorway of a tremendous cathedral. I had lost my red bathrobe somehow, but I did not feel at all embarrassed. I felt it was good to be there. A middle-aged priest whom I didn't know greeted me cordially and welcomed me by name. I was surprised at this but glad. There was something really wonderful about this.

"Father," I said, "I think I left my clothes in the sacristy. I will go down and get dressed." He did not seem astonished at my scanty attire, but he thought it might be good if I had my way.

I seemed to know the place. I made my way through a garden of tall white lilies and tall white rose bushes and other pure white flowers. I was surprised to see them growing there. It occurred to me that this was a church that planted its own flowers. It was an enormous church and evidently needed hundreds of dollars worth of flowers every day for its various altars. I passed through this garden and came to a large marble balustrade. There was nobody there. I went down a flight of stairs and crossed through another garden. These flowers were all red and pink. Their perfume was wonderful. They were not tall flowers. They grew in little beds or plots and there were paths leading through them. I felt them brush the calves of my legs as I passed. On one side was a wheelbarrow heaped with earth and flowers.

I made my way to the sacristy. I looked around in that tremendous and magnificent place, but nowhere could I find any clothes that belonged to me.

I made my way back to the priest at the entrance and told him I wanted to go to eleven o'clock mass and that I must go home and get some decent clothes.

"Oh no," he said, "You can't do that, Father Doherty. You will miss Mass altogether if you leave."

"Do you have a five o'clock mass here," I asked.

"We have masses all the time," he answered. "Why don't you pick out a cassock in the sacristy. That will cover your scanty clothing."

"Thanks," I said and dashed away.

Something had happened to the front garden. There was a rubber fence in front of it. I managed to get one leg over it, and I was straddling it when a boy helped me to lift the other leg. I went through the lilies and the roses with a feeling of great exaltation. There was a wire fence at the other end. I had some difficulty getting over that. Again a boy helped me get both legs over.

But I found myself, to my great surprise, lying in a concrete tank half filled with water. I hadn't noticed this tank before, but I wasn't too surprised to find myself swimming in it. I thought this was a good way to irrigate the garden. The water must have been put in it a few minutes before.

I got back on to the marble balustrade and there were many men and women there. Nobody seemed shocked or scandalized seeing a man in his wet shorts here in this beautiful cathedral. Some looked at me with smiles, some nodded, nobody snickered. I went down a flight of stairs and through the red garden. There were no difficulties there.

Again I had that sensation of rich aroma. I pulled the scent of the flowers into my lungs. Coming out I forgot the way to the sacristy and I was running down a long marble incline or ramp, not a stairway. A wide path that led down a long, long way. I kept running effortlessly, feeling happier and happier as I neared the altar.

When I was halfway down, a group of priests or bishops came in a solemn procession across the pathway and disappeared up a flight of stairs to the altar, which I could not see. They were all wearing white vestments that shone like the fir trees in Combermere when the sun smiles upon the snow that covers them. I was thrilled and awed by this procession and elated that I had arrived in time for mass.

Then I stopped short, for there was a group of people, priests perhaps, in black cassocks, who stood directly in front of me as though they might be on the gospel side of the altar. They knew me and called to me with joy. They began to dance up and down. One did a hand spring, another turned somersault after somersault. Some were doing a Russian dance. And they kept calling to me . . . "Father Doherty, Father Doherty!"

Now perhaps this dream is significant. Perhaps it isn't. I

don't know. But I interpret it to mean that I was closer to heaven in the Winslow Memorial Hospital than I knew. Perhaps it was St. Peter who recognized me at the gate of the church and passed me on in my crazy wardrobe. And perhaps it was the prayers and the masses that you offered for me that kept me there on the marble ramp, and stopped me from going to the waiting saints.

How do I know it wasn't?

But there are two heavens, and I still live in heaven on earth!

With all my blessings,
Father Eddie.

8

YELLOW BUG POUSTINIA

To those who seek him in the desert, God is a royal host and a tender father. He treats his guests with fantastic generosity and care. And he gives them gifts more precious than those he gives the highest angels.

One day while I was walking with him on the lava-black and sovereign-yellow carpet he had stretched for me across the Arizona desert—a wrinkled and lumpy texture of sand and lava-dust and sun-seared sage and cactus—I thanked him for a jade-like bit of petrified wood I had picked up.

"You kept this three or four billions of years, right here, for me?" I asked.

"If you knew what treasures I have stored up for you and all other men in heaven," he said, "you would not think highly of anything so material as this."

Another voice cut into our conversation. "Eye has not seen, nor ear heard, nor has it entered into the heart of man, what things God has prepared for those who love him."

St. Paul! I run into the little man everywhere these days.

I said hello to him and forgot him because of the beauty of another piece of petrified wood lying at my feet. But all the time I was examining the stone I kept tasting the beauty of his words. Suddenly I realized he was gone—and the Lord with him! I could imagine God's winking at the apostle and gesturing to him to "leave the poor child alone with his earthly treasure; and pray that he grows up."

I stood a long time, staring at my field of treasures and at the wide, wide, wide, serenely lovely sky.

Every day, or nearly every day, for the next few weeks, I went to the desert to amass the riches of the Lord. Always one of the girls from the Casa drove me there. And while I hunted, uphill and downhill and across the valleys and down other hills, the girls stayed in the car using the vehicle as a poustinia. May Carpenter, a friend of Madonna House, thus describes her day spent in a "cabin poustinia" in Combermere:

A poustinia is a place in the desert
They tell me, dear Lord.
Where one is silent in solitude,
To pray to you, O holy one
To ask for your forgiveness
For the things we may have done
Willfully or unknowingly,
As only you can tell.
But I find this little house, O Lord,
Not barren as the desert sands
But warm and filled with love,
Because You are right at hand
So close, so very close
That if I reached out my hand
I'm sure you'd clasp it tightly
As only you, Lord, can!

The girls, Theresa Marsey, Kathleen O'Shea and Kathy McVady, felt that the front seat of their old station wagon was also "warm and filled with love." If they ventured to help me find what I sought, it was only for a few moments.

Then they scurried back to the car and the Bible and the other books they had brought along with them.

The dog, the crazy black and white monster who pretends to guard the Casa and chases all the passing trucks away from it—romped up and down the hills with me, barked at everything including a low-hanging cloud, and scratched up half the territory with his claws. I stacked my loot in piles, marking each one with a clean white handkerchief. When I thought I had enough piles, I blew a whistle. Sometimes one of the girls came running to me to carry the rocks to the car. My nurses do not permit me to lift anything heavier than a corned beef sandwich on rye, with maybe a little mustard—not too much.

Sometimes a girl filled two or three cardboard boxes and carried them in her arms. My last piles were never more than half a mile away from the car. Well, hardly ever. The girls enjoyed it. It was good for their health and their morale. And what it did for their complexions you wouldn't believe!

Theresa, the Casa director, usually put all the stones into one big box. And this box she carried on her head.

I liked that at first, but after a while I noticed she was making extra work for me. Every once in awhile she would stop on her way up some hill and holler, "Father D!" That meant I would have to climb a little faster until I reached her. Then she would show me a stone too good to pass by and ask me to pick it up for her and put it in the box she still held on her head. So, as usual, I had to do all the heavy work.

There came a rainy February day when I decided to stay away from the ever-tempting hills and write a column or two for Restoration. I was sitting at my desk in front of my typewriter, and staring at some notes I had written. I could get no inspiration from them. I could hardly read them. "No man sprints with his legs in splints." Something like that. What did it mean? I felt a depression of spirits which may have been what the Lord wanted.

My friend Clarence O'Neill came just then, in a new yellow Volkswagen bug, and invited me to visit a part of Arizona I had missed.

"Let's see what the Lord hath wrought," quoth he.

So I got into his car and we rode for more than three hundred miles, through mountains and forests and oases and deserts; and I too learned that the front seat of a car can really be a poustinia, even when the machine is doing a sober steady seventy, and neither the driver nor his pal in the suicide seat have very much to say.

The sun welcomed us as Clarence, a retired railroad engineer, gave the bug full throttle. And God's illimitable territory rolled away from us even as it rolled toward us. Glorious sunshine and no wind. But there were rain clouds far away on the left. They sat in a long pew, like so many black-robed nuns, and wept for the sins of the people. I could almost hear them. "Lord have mercy; Lord have mercy; Lord have mercy!"

In the middle of Holbrook Clarence turned right; and I began to notice the things that men had wrought . . . a bewildering and baffling maze of electric neon light and plain ordinary painted wooden signs . . . each trying to tell us or sell us something we didn't want . . . (one sign offered "Sleep for Sale; $3 a night")

Roads, bridges, houses, stores, church steeples,

restaurants, cafes, dining rooms, eat shops, snackeries, motels, hotels, inns, movie houses, hospitals, a jail, and a thousand kinds of hurrying vehicles—including a long, long freight that Clarence watched with interest.

"Heading for Snow Flake," he said. "Mormon town. Mormons always bring beauty to a community. Wide streets. Trees. Gardens. Snow Flake is as pretty as its name."

Fine rain fell on the windshield, but no snow flakes. We hurried on to Show Low. Then the snow flakes came. And heavy rain. And dense fog. Clarence slowed to a stodgy sixty until the fog lifted. "Town got its name on the turn of a card," he said. "Big rancher lost all his money to a gambler. Then all his cattle. Then his entire herd of horses. In desperation he hazarded the entire ranch, including the oil and mineral rights, against what he had lost. One card.

" 'High or low!' the gambler asked. The rancher lost to high cards. He said 'Low.' Gambler cut a trey and smiled. Rancher shut his eyes, drew a card, and prayed, 'Showlow!' He showed a deuce."

We went on. Heavy snow. Reckless winds. Great pine forests, fruitful plains, patches of desert set with Joshua trees that reminded me of the prophets, one or two or three arms upraised to admonish, to praise the Lord, to bless, to curse, to prophesy. We went through curving roads, down into green valleys and new sunlight and cloud shadows that hit the sides of hills, shadows that created an amateur twilight. We passed mine shafts, slag piles, and signs that failed to frighten Clarence:—Icy spots, 16 miles. Slippery when wet, 13 miles . . . . Caution! Sharp curves.

A voice began to speak to me. Not Clarence's. A voice without sound. It came from behind one of my desert windows—the one that always sticks. I had forgotten those mysterious glassless aids to inner vision. I always forget them, yet they are always with me.

"Caution, all you who feed on the flesh of swine, the seven deadly sins. Slow down! Your road is filled with icy spots! It is slippery indeed!"

Clarence spoke. "Father Eddie! The desert where Christ was tempted by the devil—did you see it . . . was it anything like this?"

"Something like this," I answered. "But there was nothing green there. Just rocks, and dust and frightful heat. Sterile waste land. The devil was at home there. He loves sterility—and sterile people."

I gazed through the rain-splashed windows of the car at the surrounding mountains. Gray. Black. Brown. Grim. Solemn. I turned them immediately into a community of ancient anchorites.

I looked at them then through one of my desert windows. And I beheld mad throngs of people running toward them and heard some of them crying out in panic and despair: "Peaks, crack and crumble! Send down your avalanches! Bury us! Crush us! Hide us from the holy wrath of God!"

I shut the window hurriedly, but for a long time as the car sped down into the sunlight and the wind and the dust around the Roosevelt dam, the screams of those men and women echoed and re-echoed in my heart.

I exclaimed about the blue water and the blue sky and all the colors in the clouds. Clarence talked about the dam, one of the great things men had wrought. And I picked up again the voice that sounded outside that window that looks at heaven.

"All the beauty you have seen today," it began, "the Lord created. He made you too. And Clarence. He made all the millions of billions of people who have lived. He is the true father of every one. Your parents did not make you. They did not give you life. They could not. Only God gives life. Neither your mother nor your father could fashion so much as one of your eyelashes.

"Only God Almighty can enter into an egg, once it has been fertilized, to work his miracle of birth. The egg is his workshop, his studio, his holy sanctuary. He labors there constantly, in women, fish, birds, insects, and beasts—and in the seeds and buds of trees and plants—to bring more beauty, more perfection to his world. His work is always perfect, though he does not always have the proper material to work on. So when an infant is born blind or crippled or retarded or malformed or afflicted with some dread disease, someone is sure to curse and say, 'If there be a God in Heaven, how could he be so cruel?' Yet a million perfect children can be born without a single voice being raised to acknowledge the miracle, or to praise his holy name.

"This is the work God loves—God the creator of all things! He has a divine love for every little body and for every little soul he blesses with his care. He has a destiny for each one and a common goal for all. The goal is heaven.

"And it may be said he has a dream for each and every one. But, alas, the world is full of the broken dreams of God—dreams intended to come true in the eternal paradise his Son bought for us with his life.

"Man has no self-made or self-earned power to create. But he does have the power—ironically—to defy the will of

God, to debase, to pollute, to damage, and to destroy. He
has the power to invade the holy sanctuary of the womb and
ruthlessly maim or kill God's work of love, God's dream of
everlasting happiness for one of his little 'might have
beens!' "

We started back to Winslow, up through snow and ice,
and through new mountain ranges and new stands of pines.
The voice I had listened to was silent. But the wheels of the
car had taken up the frantic chant heard in the monastic
mountains. "Fall on us! Bury us! Hide us from the wrath of
God!"

Indeed one can have a poustinia in the front seat of a
car—even such a little one as Clarence's yellow bug.

9

RAPHAEL'S OASIS

The Canadian sun stayed just outside the windows of St. Raphael's—our lovely oasis in the desert, here in Combermere. It was, I fancied, a beggar too shy to knock, too timid to approach. I was glad of that for I had no idea of welcoming him into the place that day.

St. Raphael's is a place that Ali Baba and the Forty Thieves would have delighted to despoil. It is filled with beauty and with grace and with the benevolence of God. Ordinarily we want the sun to shine into our windows, to reveal all the things with which God, through the boundless generosity of many people, has so abundantly blessed us. But not this day.

The table close to me was covered with a confusion of sparkling jewels. Amethysts, rubies, garnets, topazes, emeralds, diamonds, sapphires, and ropes and strings of pearls and beads—a tumbled, jumbled, glittering rainbow—the spoils of many palaces.

It would be a shame to let the sun shine on them and show them up as so many bits of paste and pretense. (Sometimes we too shrink from the thought of living in light—the glaring pitiless truth.)

Some of that jewelry needed repair; all of it needed sorting. A woman worked with it, hour after hour, patient as a mother with a retarded child. She matched necklaces and bracelets and earrings and pendants. She put some in this box, some in that.

Many things will be given away. Many will be sold in our

gift shop. Some will be bought by visitors to Madonna House and the money will help maintain our missions here and abroad. Some will go, this Christmas, to young girls who never dreamed they would have such treasures in their hands, to their older sisters, to their mothers, perhaps, and possibly to some old women who haven't had anything "so nice" since they were married.

The jewelry is a sacred trust to the woman who bent over it. Her touch was a caress; for, in a sense, she was touching the love and the bounty of Christ and his care for "even the least of these."

St. Raphael's is one of the noblest buildings in the Madonna House Apostolate. I was visiting it in order to write something about it. Bill Jakali, a staff worker, designed it and helped to put it up. Bill couldn't tell you the difference between a hammer and a wedge when he first came to Madonna House. Now he is an architect. He is also one of our expert carpenters. Likewise, he is one of our best artists. The desert has given him many gifts!

The monks in the desert worked as they prayed and fasted. They relied on God and pious pilgrims for all they needed. Food. Drink. Clothing. And a fair share in the love of God and man. The visitors sometimes brought "extras." Scraps of leather. Rare woods. Jars of beads or little stones to be turned into mosaics. Tools. Brushes and paints. Well-scraped hides to be covered with words of wisdom and compassion. Broken pieces of glass in many colors to be magically fashioned into windows for a church.

The desert of St. Raphael's is like that. No monks here, though. Only men and women, all of them artists; all trying to be saints; all working hard and spending long hours at their tasks; all working with one supreme thought—to serve

God well and give him praise and thanks and glory and to restore his kingdom to him.

The pilgrims come. And the caravans come. No camels now. Just trucks, some bigger than freight cars, each filled with gifts for Madonna House to dispose of.

Triumphant generals came back to Rome with the loot of conquered cities, carrying far less joy than the littlest and least-laden of these trucks.

"It all comes from Our Lady," we say. "She is our shopper, our buyer, our provider, our manager, our mother. She sends us everything we need for ourselves; and an abundance to give away. Also she gives us money for our missions."

A painting on the wall distracted me. I left my typewriter and stood in front of the picture a long time. It is one of Joan Bryant's. I could see the artist outside in the full splendor of the sun. She was sitting on a stool in front of an easel. And she was wrapping a beautiful part of the world in a little piece of canvas to keep it forever! Beauty everywhere inside. Beauty everywhere outside.

I wandered through St. Raphael's, upstairs and down, like a tourist in the Louvre. Downstairs, Ed Wildgen, one of our working guests, was finishing a candle. The tables around him were covered with candles. Some were, like Joseph's coat, of many colors. The tables were like altars set for mass, waiting for some acolyte to come in with a lighted match.

I picked up a candle and saw that it bore flowers from the Holy Land.

Eventually I went back to my typewriter. But I could not write. The woman sorting the jewelry had distracted me, fascinated me (she always does). I watched her, both of us silent.

Suddenly she was handling a chain of tiny lightning flashes; and just as suddenly I wanted it, whatever it might be. I have a vow of poverty. I am not supposed to want anything at all. But this I not only wanted, I had to have.

"A rosary," the woman said. "Iridescent crystals. Somebody must have paid a lot of money for this."

There was, I suspected, tragedy of some kind on those lovely beads. Maybe they had been given to a little girl for her first communion. Maybe they had been given to a bride. What had happened to the little girl? What had happened to the bride? Why did someone send us this glitter of ecstasy and glory?

"Do you want it?" the woman asked.

I took it from her without a word and stared at it in the same way I had looked at the array of candles. I put away my typewriter, went across the road to my room in Madonna House, then visited the chapel to say the joyful mysteries of the new Rosary, *my* new Rosary!

As I kissed the beautifully wrought golden crucifix, I began to feel more than a trifle foolish. What was I doing here in a shadowy chapel with a feminine rosary in my fist? Me! Butch Doherty's son! Young Butch, "the tough guy from Chicago!" I felt embarrassed by all the angels skipping up and down between my fingers. I brushed them off. And thrust the beads into my pocket. I made a bow, Eastern-rite style, to the ikons on either side of the altar and went back to my room.

"The seed must be divine, the flower human." The words

tormented me for days. For many days. They haunted me until I heard the voice.

"Don't you know that the divine seed is the will of God, the grace of God, the love God has for his creatures? It falls on good soil or on rocks or shrubbery or sand. And it falls into a heart . . . !"

My stupid brain began to understand that the will of God, the Father, was the divine seed from which the flower grew and flourished—to die upon a man-made cross and fill the world with holy and enduring fragrance! I said the glorious mysteries and went down to dinner. A young and very pretty girl was sitting at my table. "I'm Mary," she said. "Will you consecrate me after dinner, Father?"

I was about to say only bishops were consecrated and that it took three other bishops to do it. But she didn't give me time. "I want to be a slave of Jesus through Mary," she explained.

"Gladly," I said. Such slaves have it easy. They consecrate themselves. I'll be your sponsor, your witness, and the one who gives the slave away—like a bride's father at a big society wedding."

No chrisms are needed. There is no laying on of hands. There is no pomp and ceremony. Only two candles smiling up at the ikon of the Immaculate, and a priest with a stole around his neck. One has only to mean with all her heart and soul the words of consecration; and she belongs forever to Jesus through Our Lady!

After supper we went upstairs to the chapel, the girl and I. She knelt and said the solemn words that needed to be said. I blessed her.

And then I passed the crystal beads down around her head and watched the cherubim and seraphim flashing their ecstasy with a chain of tiny lightnings.

Divine seed had fallen into fertile soil. And Our Lady had a new bright flower in her garden.

10

BODY OF CHRIST. AMEN

When the Bedouin angels, encamped in the desert of my priesthood, offer this day to the Lord, let them remember the hollyhocks. Especially the hollyhocks.

They can forget the red leaf that fluttered down to me in the woods, the first red leaf of autumn. They can forget my delight in the multitude of mushrooms and in the sight of a red-winged blackbird flashing across my path. They can forget those monkey-faced pansies, scrambling at the feet of the stone wall in a riot of purple and yellow splendor. They can forget the marigolds and the snapdragons and all the other flowers in the garden and the shameless and beautiful way they traded favors with the bees. But they must not forget the hollyhocks, that row of long-legged, slender beauties, drunk with the glory of the Lord and with the beauty he bestowed upon them.

This is the feast of the Transfiguration.

"The divine Master took Peter, James, and John and led them to a high mountain—Mount Thaber, near Nazareth. While praying there, he became transfigured; his face glowed with the effulgence of the sun and his garments became white as snow. The splendor of his divinity penetrated his human body and was seen in his human person. Jesus appeared in his splendor and glory as the Son of God and the eternal Word."

At the mass this morning I concelebrated with Father Briere and several other Latin-rite priests. And I could not help but feel something of the glory the three apostles saw.

Father Briere spoke of the glory of the Lord that can be seen in the face of every man and woman—if a man but looks to see. As he spoke, one of my desert windows swung open and I saw the face of Christ on the good Samaritan as he carried the wounded man to the inn.

I had never thought of Christ as the good Samaritan, the good neighbor, the only one who took pity on the poor man beaten by robbers and left to die. Why? Perhaps because it was so obvious!

But now the thought possessed me. It was a distraction. But what is a distraction to me? My mind is like a weed by the wayside. It collects every blast of dust; it shivers with every wind; it droops with too much sun; it lifts its head to every drop of rain.

Christ was a good Samaritan. I was another Christ. But was I another good Samaritan? Did I love my neighbor as Christ did? Would I go out of my way—and out of my pocket—to help anyone? Was there anything in my stingy old heart except that clump of spiny cactus? Perhaps there was. A patch of poison ivy!

Before I quite realized it, it was time for communion. And then I was two people. I was the good Samaritan treating the wounds of the victim of the robbers. I was giving him the wine of heaven and the healing oil of love. And I was at the same time the one who so sadly needed that blessed treatment.

Again and again I thanked Our Lady and Our Lord for giving me the priesthood, the supreme gift of God!

Because I have some difficulty in standing for more than a few minutes at a time, my archbishop has permitted me to say mass sitting down. I am allowed to sit down during most of the Roman mass. Always, there is a soft chair ready for me when I come into the chapel. (They really pamper me.)

(The desert of the priesthood is not harsh, nor austere, nor dreadful in any way. And I think it has more life and love in it than any other place that shelters love and life.)

Father Briere asked me to give communion to the congregation and he adjusted my chair to make the task less arduous for me.

Then, with that window still turned on the Holy Land, I was the good Samaritan treating the wounds of many others—all beaten by many kinds of robbers and left to die on the highway. I attended to their wounds one by one; healing them one by one.

Here was a girl, eager hands stretched toward me.

"Body of Christ," I said and took a host from the ciborium and placed it on her palm.

Here was a young man who knelt at my feet and opened his mouth.

"Body of Christ," I said and placed the host on his tongue.

"Body of Christ."

"Body of Christ."

"Body of Christ."

The window slammed shut, then opened again and I could see Our Lady giving Joseph the child to kiss.

"Body of Christ."

"Body of Christ."

"Body of Christ."

They came and went, men and women and children. And wonder grew in me. And delight.

I was like Our Lady. I could put the child Jesus in the

hands of the people or in their mouths. And perhaps even into their hearts! How did this mystery come about?

I shut the window gently and tried to open the one that sticks—the one that opens on heaven. It still stuck. I wanted to say thanks. I wanted to say, "I love you, God." But, as I said, the window stuck. I tugged at it, but it wouldn't budge. Well, if you can't peer into heaven to see God and talk to him, you can always find him on earth. So I continued with the work—and the privilege—of a priest.

"Body of Christ."

Wonder and delight became a sort of ecstasy in the repetition and the rapture of the name. It was as though I were signing to angelic music, singing the most glorious of all litanies.

"Body of Christ. Body of Christ. Body of Christ."

And it was like drinking rich sweet wine.

The spell was still on me as I ventured outside to talk to the Lord and thank him for this new blessing. I saw him in a pink wild rose, the last wild rose of summer; and I was sure then that I would also find him in the first red leaf of fall. I saw him in a pine cone and held him a long time in my hands. The cone has more marvels than man has found in the moon.

I went across the bridge to Hermit Island where the new chapel is rising. The tall pine trees stood all around it, arms linked like people in our chapel holding hands as they say "Our Father." He was there, blessing them, blessing the building, blessing the builders.

I wanted to thank him for all the gifts he has showered on me in the past two years, but instead of thanking him I began to complain. He has had surprises for me every day, big and little tokens of his love. But I never have any surprises for him. What can I say that he has not, since long before time began, foreknew that I would say? What can I do that he has not always anticipated?

I came back toward Madonna House and stayed some little while in the garden made for St. Joseph. I saw him in the flowers and in the grass and in the plum trees and in the vines. And I saw him in the people passing by.

And then I saw that chorus-line of hollyhocks. And I saw myself there as well as him!

The hollyhocks were as drunk as I was. They swayed and swooned in the wind, exhibiting their gratitude and their love and their adoration in the only way they could. They capered and danced to show their joy, careless of any sourpuss or critic who might think them delirious or indecent.

They adored the Lord openly and with all their lovely bodies—all their little buttons and all their bell-shaped pink and crimson faces; the only flowers anywhere so gloriously unashamed to love!

It was because of the wind, of course. They were the only flowers exposed to it.

"The wind of the Holy Spirit," a voice said silently. "The wind of Pentecost."

My wife Catherine came walking toward me.

"Body of Christ."

"I am not hollyhock," I said. "I thought I was just a cactus. I'm not. I'm an uninhibited hollyhock."

"Are you feeling ill?" she asked. "Why don't you go to your room and lie down?"

I went upstairs to my room and turned on the air-conditioner that Tom Gibson, God rest his generous soul, gave me so many years ago. A great wind filled the room;

but I am still waiting for the wind of Pentecost to whistle through and through me—so that I may offer beauty to the Lord.

Let the Bedouin angels, when they take this day up to heaven, kneel at Our Lady's feet and beg her to send me the wind I need so terribly, the wind of the Holy Spirit, the wind of God, her Spouse.

11

THE HEALING OF MY I

Almost everybody knows that heaven has at least one murderer-thief—St. Dismas, who was crucified with Christ. But how many know that heaven also has billions of expert burglars and uses them everyday and every night?

I didn't know this until I went to St. Michael's Hospital for an operation on my eye. The more I got to thinking about it, the more I was convinced that God really has a whole army of burglars working for him constantly. These, of course, are the angels. They get in any house, in any mind, in any heart. They even got into my desert cell in the hospital and left a dream behind them.

I don't know how many angels there were. How many does it take to carry a dream down from heaven and across the desert sands? I can't say whether they carry this dream on the backs of camels or whether they floated it along the way or how they managed to get it to me. I was asleep. They must have come through the window that always sticks, the window that looks into heaven. I can't see any other source of entry.

I don't know whether they came through the window like light through a pane of glass or whether they forced the window open. I never could do anything like that myself. But angels—they can do anything.

We started out from Combermere, Catherine and Father Briere and I, as though we were going to a picnic. My doctor, W.P. Callahan, is reputed to be the best eye surgeon in the world and everybody who knew him said it would be a picnic.

One of my correspondents, the lady that lives in Dubuque, told me such an operation was nothing at all. Absolutely nothing. "My mother had this operation done on both eyes," she said, "and within two or three years she saw almost as well as ever. The operation is really nothing."

So in the spirit of picnicking we moved the car off the road in a place called Eels Creek where the Province of Ontario has placed a lot of tables and benches. A beautiful rustic section of this most beautiful country in the world. We had a picnic dinner there and listened to the creeking of the eels and then went on for a picnic of the eyes.

It may seem strange but I remember almost nothing of the operation. The dream takes up all my meditation. I was so unaware of what had happened to my eyes that I was shocked when someone asked me if I had had the stitches taken out. I didn't know I had stitches in my eye. I didn't feel them being stitched.

Really the eye was nothing, although it took a lot of time and patience and much attention. The dream was everything.

The dream began with a man sitting at a desk in a room. He was all alone. His little boy was calling him through the door. "Daddy, can I come in?"

"You know the rules," the man said, "go to school."

"But I want to come in and kiss you goodbye, Daddy."

"Go to school." The man was very angry. "You heard me. Go to school. Don't bother me again—ever."

His wife called to him from behind the door. "But darling, he only wanted to kiss you goodbye." "Don't butt in," the man shouted. "Butt out. Let me alone. You know the rules too."

"Yes dear," she said. And then there was silence inside the room and outside.

The man, I saw, was an author. He had almost finished a new book. His hand-written pages were lying there before him, making quite a pile. He stood brooding, pen in hand. He looked at the door and threw down the pen. He took up the manuscript and threw it on the floor. He kicked it around. He sat down suddenly and shook with self-anger— such a weakening of anger that he clutched at the desk for support.

"So this is me," he said aloud. "This is actually me shouting at my little boy to go away, shouting at my wife. This is actually me, Benedict Shamokin Davis! What has happened to me in the last ten years?"

In my dream I not only saw Benedict Shamokin Davis, I became Benedict Shamokin Davis. I was a famous literary star. I was supposed to know all about women. The critics said I knew more about women than any other male author that ever lived.

They said I knew more about making love than any other writer. But I sat here day after day shut in that fussy room from 8:30 to 1:30 writing, writing, writing, letting my thoughts go strictly on the white paper beneath my pen. I hadn't said a civil word to my wife in years. I hadn't kissed my little boy in many days.

I was a lover; but only on paper. I was a fraud. I was a cheater. I was a blithering idiot.

This morning at breakfast I saw the first white hair in my wife's head as she bent over to pour coffee and a beautiful line came to me: "Snowline of her youth, the beginning of the end of her dancing days." I didn't say anything to Eunice. I hadn't paid her a compliment since Lord knows when. I saved the line for my book.

What a silly ass I am. I put Eunice in every book I write. I put my love for her on every page. Yet I never say a word about it to her.

I remember another gracious line I wrote in some book or other: "Hand makes love to hand and eye to eye before ever lips make love to lips."

I have written much more about women's hands and the art of holding hands. I have written much about the eyes of women and what men see in them. I have also written much about rubbing noses. I used to rub noses with Eunice when we were young and foolish. When I first saw her, her nose was full of freckles. It was the most beautiful nose God ever put on a woman. So I rubbed noses with her. I rubbed all the freckles off. Now—now I can't tell you what her nose looks like.

She used to call me "Davie-Davie" in those days. Once she looked up with shining eyes and called me "Mr. Eskimo."

I don't deserve a woman like that. She deserves something better than a man like me. I must leave her for her own sake.

I must get away from her. I must abandon her only to save her youth. What can I do? Where can I go? What does it matter where I go so long as I disappear?

I will find somebody to replace me. Someone who will give her all the babies she ever wanted. Someone who will dance with her. Someone who will take her wherever she wants to go. Someone who will spend the rest of his life devoted to her and to her children.

Mr. Benedict Shamokin Davis, famous author, threw a pen across the room and went through a secret door down into his garage where he tinkered with his grass mower for a long time. He knew that Eunice would come in as she always did when he was gone, to look over what he had written. He wanted her to know that he had left her because he loved her.

He spent a longer time than he wanted to with the machine because he was afraid to come back and face her, but finally he made the effort. She was in his room as he had expected she would be. She had read the manuscript. She was holding it in her hands. She was white. And she was shaking as though she had the chills and fever.

"Benedict," she said, "you are a hard man to live with, but if you leave me I will die. I just can't do without you."

"I have already left you," he said, "but I am making provisions for you. I am sending someone here to take care of you and Benedict, Jr. Somebody who will love you very much."

She drew away from him.

"You are crazy," she said. "You are crazy."

"No," he said, "not now. I am sending you Davie-Davie."

She came closer to him, looking up at him curiously. Suddenly her eyes were shining. She held up her face to him.

"Mr. Eskimo," she said, "welcome home."

This was the dream. A real short story. I was excited and delighted. It was good to be writing a short story again. I had written many in my youth but for a long, long time I had been writing books. This was the first short story that I had ever formed itself perfectly in my mind—beginning, climax, and end. This was worth my right eye—even if I lost it. This was worth anything, this beautiful story, this dream.

I woke with the spell of the dream still on me and wondered how it had come to me.

It was only then that I began to suspect some angel had burgled into my room, into my mind, into my heart, and left without leaving any trace of his entry.

I was quite certain the dream had come from God and that it had some sort of message for me. But days passed and I didn't know what the message was.

I have never neglected any wife of mine. I have always made love to **her**, publicly and in private. It could not be meant to teach me how to love Catherine.

Eventually the answer came. It was meant to show me how to love God. For years I have written about him and to him. Perhaps I had neglected him in the same way Benedict Shamokin Davis had neglected his wife and child.

If you can't rub noses with the Lord, rub elbows with his friends. Whatever you do to the least of his brethren you do to him.

Love everybody; man, woman, and child. Love them with your hands, with your eyes, any way they need to be loved. Love them for the love of God, so that the love of God shines through you. Love them and make sure they know you love them.

I not only had an operation on my sight, but on my insight also.

12

THE BIRDS OF JOY

Pink! Plink! Plunk! Birds of Joy! Plank!

That, I think, is the only logical way to begin this praise-applying, love-supplying, never dying bit of pure and priceless prose. The pink, plink, plunk belongs to a couple of wandering minstrels. Only the plank is mine; and I need it to build a program of thanksgiving to the Lord.

A tall young man with long hair and an extremely long guitar sauntered into my particular desert here in Combermere a week or so ago and sang me a few songs before he left. His name is Paul Grady. He and his friend Stuart Crisco wrote the words and music. The words he wrote down for me. Listen while he sings them:

"I'm just sittin' here, drinkin' and thinkin'
No, I don't feel like jokin' with the boys.
Yes, I'm feeling rather lonely
And I'm growin' somewhat tired of all the noise."
CHORUS: Oh, birds of joy, please fly down to my shoulders
And grab ahold of my old threadbare coat
And spread your wings and lift me to the heavens.
Happy skyward will I rise forever more.
I left home—now was it March or April?
Left alone, to make the wind go still.
But the wind I know is mightier than I,
So I ask You, Spirit in the sky—CHORUS.
Now the train I'm ridin' rolls along

And it rolls in spite of all that must go wrong.
Like the train that rolls through snow or rain,
Stoke the fire and let me whistle again."

When he had finished singing about the birds of joy and
the spirit in the wind, he encased his ornate instrument in a
case as big as a coffin and made ready to "hit the road and
hitch a hike." Madonna House girls made him a lunch to
take along and he went singing happily away.

A few days later three of us went rolling through the rain
and the light snow and the happy frisky winds, each with
birds of joy nestling on our shoulders. I was going to my
eye-surgeon again. My seeing-nurse Marian and Thurston
Smith, who drove the car, were my companions.

We returned in time to celebrate Canada's Thanksgiving
Day here in Madonna House. And I am arranging today,
Thanksgiving Day, to send flocks and flocks of birds of joy
wrapped in fleecy white clouds—if I can find any to sing to
the Lord songs of praise and love and adoration and hymns
that will find mercy for all of us here below.

Now, of course, the logical window to open when I release
the birds is the one that looks at heaven all day and all night
too, but it continues to be stubborn. It still sticks. So I'll
open the window that frowns on the gray sands and the
wastelands of my life. The birds may find a lot of friends
along my trail and take them along. Happy skyward will
they rise. And when each cloud is opened, the joyful birds
will sing.

Now isn't that a pretty dish to set before my king?

Pretty yes, but not pretty enough. Never pretty enough.
And that's the drop of gall in all my honey. I will never be

able to give Him the joy I want to give Him.

The joy he fills me with is divine. The joy I send up to him is only human—and I don't always send it up. Nor do I always share it as I should. Lord have mercy. Lord have mercy. Lord have mercy.

The birds of joy were singing in the woodlands on either side of the road as our auto sped along—woods blazing with scarlet and crimson and orange and pale gold—woods that made a fellow think of the burning bush that Moses found on the mountain. (And the voice of the Lord bade him, "Take off your shoes, for the place is holy.") We didn't hear even a twitter. We didn't catch the flash of a single wing. But David himself sang to us as he bade all creation to praise the king of all.

"Praise the Lord from the earth, you sea monsters and all you depths. Fire and hail, snow, ice, mist, and stormy winds that fulfill his word; you mountains and all you hills, you fruit trees and all you cedars—and all you winged fowls."

The altar in our Madonna House chapel was decorated with red leaves this morning and with all the fruits of the harvest—including the humble carrot. And public thanks were offered for all the blessings, all the graces, and all the mercies the Lord has showered upon Madonna House during the year.

The mass—well, what is the mass anyway but birds of joy flying upward in praise of God and in petition for all His friends? Every day is a thanksgiving day for the priest. Before he starts the divine liturgy the Byzantine priest, bowing low before the ikon of Christ, says in solemn adoration:

"We cry out to you in thanksgiving, you our Savior filled all things with joy when you came to save the world."

And the Roman priest after he has consecrated the Bread and Wine says, with his hands extended wide:

"Father, calling to mind the death your son endured for our salvation, his glorious resurrection and ascension into heaven and ready to greet him when he comes again, we offer you in thanksgiving this holy and living sacrifice!"

Birds of joy indeed—offering God to God!

During the mass, and after it, I sent a few birds skyward to thank God for the new vision that has come to my right eye. Dr. Callahan, who peeled the cataract out of that blue orb, has fitted it with a new lens. So this battered old camera has two lenses. They do not work in harmony as they should. They may get together in time; but their teamwork is most confusing now. The left eye, which still has a cataract in it, sees ordinary things. The right sees extraordinary things.

Color is just color to the left. To the right it is a miracle of beauty. I looked at an old striped rug with my left eye yesterday. It was just a rug some upstairs maid had thrown in my path (in a purely feminine attempt to trip me). How rugged is my upstairs desert cell!

Today I saw it with my right eye—through the lens prescribed for me. And it was one of the most beautiful rugs I had ever noticed. It glowed. It was as clean and bright as though it had been washed in every television soap commercial. Honestly, it was as lovely as a strip of red and blue and green and yellow flowers in our garden.

They are not really two eyes. Rather they are a sort of hook-and-eye combination. The eye doesn't always meet the hook, nor the hook meet the eye.

All during the day I sent up flocks of birds, singing Hosannas and asking for mercy.

Toward the evening I sent up the biggest flock of all—to thank the shepherd of good shepherds for making me a pastor in this far-off desert.

Once, just before I was ordained, I begged the Lord never to pastorize me. I had come into the priesthood in my 79th year, when most of the pastors of my age had long since retired or died, and I realized I wasn't fit to be even an assistant pastor's tenth assistant.

I didn't want any parish work anyway, and I said so, plainly, to the Lord. I wanted to remain here among the shifting sand dunes and the unmoving cactus, without responsibilities, without restrictions, without too many rules and regulations.

But the Lord had ideas of his own. He always does. So he gave me a tremendous parish!

Overnight his caravans arrived with hundreds of young men and maidens, wild elders, and with children. Both the living and the dead. I have never seen any of them. They have never seen me. Even their names are strange to me. But they are my people and they are dear to me.

They came with stipends, asking masses for their intentions, for their souls, for their enemies, and for their friends. Now I am their shepherd and I tend them every day.

Green pastures in the desert? And still waters? It is even so!

The birds of joy are thanking the Lord now for these my flocks. And they have instructions to remind him that my sheep are his sheep too and he should help me care for them, now and always and forever and ever. Amen.

Before I go to sleep tonight I will set free the final flock of happy birds, to thank God for all the joy he has showered on me through my relatives and friends and through his chosen lay apostles. They have pampered me for years.

There has always been a gentle hand to cook the things I like, to serve them, to bring me fresh-cut flowers, to flick my rumpled hair back from my bulging brow, to straighten my collar—even to brush the dandruff from my shoulders.

13

GOOD FRIDAY PRESENTS

The morning's clouds evidently had a bad night. Some were that give-away, tattle-gray look. Some were shrivelled and shrunk. A few were covered with mildew. Apparently some heaven-happy upstairs maid had left them out too long in the rain.

The sun took charge of the day and life became happier. The clouds put on their sheerest white. The sky donned a Mary-blue apron. And the world opened up its beautiful wardrobe. Miss Upstairs Maid, probably lonesome for the kind of life she had enjoyed on earth, threw scatter-rug clouds everywhere, hoping they might trip an angel and make him fall smack on his little harp. (In such a case she might overhear whatever he said as he crashed.) Thank heavens none of the upstairs maids in this Madonna House oasis are so mischievous or so unangelic.

It is an October day I am writing about. I remember similar days in April, for isn't April a sister of October? Variety must run in the family. Now gloom. Now brightness. Now a million fairies dancing in the tulips and the violets and the marigolds and the fat green grass. Now, on this October day yellow leaves; the crimson gold of the maples had left the woods, but there was still magnificence in God's world. Great patches of russet and rust and mustard and gold and green! Green of the eternal hills. Green of eternal hope, and love and mercy, and divine assurance.

I saw October falling apart that day, so close to my 81st

birthday; and I saw myself standing like empty trees, holding my arms up to the God of heaven and earth, trying to explain why I had no more golden leaves to sacrifice for him.

I had come back to Combermere from a visit to my seeing-eye doctor in Toronto. He had promised that within a few weeks of my surgery I would have almost perfect vision in my right eye. I returned with a temporary pair of glasses.

And I could see!

I had never been blind, though there have been times when I saw as through a veil. I had always loved God's world—what I could see of it—and I have seen more than half of it. My earliest memories are of fields of daisies and violets and wild roses and shining yellow dandelions. We lived on the northwest corner of Chicago when I was a child and there was, for miles and miles, nothing back of our house but farms and prairies—and semi-swamps where a boy could catch frogs and crayfish and an occasional snake to take to school with him. One could say it was love at first sight.

Coming home from Toronto was love at second sight. A love more overwhelming and more profound than the first. For I saw all things with new eyes.

I thought of one of those my Lord Jesus healed; the man born blind. When he looked up after the Savior had spoken he saw the full glory of God shining on him out of the eyes of a man. Who can even try to describe his emotions! How can I describe what I felt when I saw the glory of God shining on me in those October red maple mosaics?

How can I describe what it was to look at the flame of a candle—or an ordinary electric light bulb? All I can say is,

I didn't see ordinary lights. These lights were great fiery thumb prints shimmering on a wall, as though some angel had rubbed his hands in gold or scarlet powder before he touched the wall.

Sometimes the thumb print was shaped like a bishop's mitre. Sometimes it looked like a moth or a butterfly with folded wings, hanging from some impossibly beautiful twig. Sometimes it was a cobweb circle, or a doily made entirely of sunbeams.

And what can I say of the colors my peeled eye saw—and still sees? I can say only that I had never seen true colors before.

Joe Hogan, one of our staff workers, says we have surrendered to the ordinary in this Madonna House Apostolate. We do ordinary things, monotonous things, trivial everyday routine things. And we discover to our amazement and through the grace of God that we are living extraordinarily happy, interesting, and exciting lives! In other words, we sow the humdrum rain and reap the glowing rainbow.

The world is new again. And I am new. At eighty-one I am brand new! And new thoughts keep coming into my old mind.

One October day—the anniversary of Our Lady's visit to Fatima, the day she spun the sun around her little finger—I was assisting one of our priests at mass in our chapel.

I looked at the red leaves that decorated the altar, and one of my desert windows banged open. I saw the Son of God, the Son of Mary, decorating his cross on Calvary, bleeding from the raw wounds in his hands and feet, from the wounds made by thorns, from the wounds the heavy cross had made on his shoulders, from the wounds made by the Roman whip, and from the wounds inflicted when his seamless robe was torn from his sacred body. It ripped away pieces of his flesh. The robe was saturated with his sweat and his blood. It did not come loose easily.

I stared a long time out of that window, looking at Jesus, looking at the good thief crucified with him, looking at the bad thief too.

Then the window that looks on heaven, the one that always sticks whenever I try to open it, caught my attention by shaking in its frame. And I heard again the voice that never speaks.

"He is weaving a welcome carpet for you. A royal red carpet. For you and all his other friends. He stretches it out before you in joy at your approach. You can walk on it directly into paradise.

"Never, never, never before was there such a carpet made for man in heaven or on earth. And look at the diamonds and pearls woven into its divine texture by the tears of women: his mother, our most pure, Mary Magdalen whom he delivered of seven demons, Mary, the mother of James and John. And all the other women who loved—or love—him. Even the tears of Peter are in the priceless fabric. Peter, who had the heart of a child."

I returned to the cross on Golgotha and saw the good thief talking to the dying son of God. "Remember me when you come into your kingdom." This is what we now call "the Jesus prayer"—"Lord Jesus, have mercy on me, a sinner."

"This day," Jesus answers, "you will be with me in Paradise."

The man born blind saw the glory of God. The good thief

dying in agony saw the mercy of God shining in those glorious eyes! He must have thought his crucifixion a blessing he did not deserve.

I would give not only my right eye but the left one and all the rest of me, to see what that most fortunate of all thieves—of all sinners—saw in his last few moments.

Even before his feet could touch the beautiful red carpet, even before he died, he was in paradise!

In a few seconds, in a few words, a man wipes out an entire life of crime. In a few seconds, in a few words, a roughneck and repulsive sinner becomes a saint to be envied by all the world.

I remember, crazily enough, an old-time ad: "Don't envy that school girl complexion; have one of your own."

Don't envy the good thief's sudden conversion and quick entry into heaven. Have one of your own.

Would it seem absurd if I said that Mary had prayed for this momentous happening and that she never prays in vain? She wanted to give both thieves a free one-way trip to heaven. And she wanted to give her Son two saints to accompany him on his journey home. The grace was offered both thugs. They could take it or reject it. Neither God nor his mother ever interfere with the free will of man.

Jesus was giving supreme gifts too. He gave his life to his Father for us. He gave his mother to John and through John to us. And he gave John to her—John and all the rest of us.

And he wove that carpet for everyone of us, including the thief who refused. Here on earth we give the red carpet treatment to V.I.P.'s but everybody who asks for mercy, even the "bum" dying in the dirt of the street, is a V.I.P. to

God. It doesn't matter how dirty his shoes. The carpet is unrolled for him with great joy, and all the angels singing.

October died a week or so ago. It passed away quietly in its sleep and its crib was given to November. Today the snow is falling and people pray for the souls in purgatory. And priests, our Madonna House priests especially, bless every graveyard they pass by. One of them hails the dead in words of joy. "Keep shining in glory, you lucky children of the Lord!"

November is a restless month. It hurries, hurries, hurries, shortening its days as it rushes on. It is eager to get out of the way so that the world can be blessed again with Christmas.

Which makes me think—if Jesus and Mary could give us such incredibly wonderful and costly Christmas presents on Good Friday, why can't each one of us give the same kind of presents to one another for Christmas?

14

PARADOXES OF LIFE

Father Cal and I, sitting easy in our easy chairs, watched a mirage pass by. A mirage with sound. A man-made mirage stationed in this desert oasis of Madonna House through the generosity of a friend. People were scooting in front of us in gaily decorated automobiles or fancy floral floats, some were waving to us, shouting to us, or nodding their happy heads.

Now and then a band passed, led by troops of majorettes with flashing air-cooled thighs and knees that moved in lovely cadence—acting on double-duty springs.

A man and a woman sitting somewhere out of our vision explained that this was the pre-Grey Cup parade. They commented on the beauty of the floats—the hundreds or thousands of real flowers in this one, the intricate symbolism in that one—the music, and the various units in the gala march.

Thousands of sports fans **had** gathered in Vancouver, B.C., to enjoy the football classic that would be played on the morrow, come rain or sleet or snow; the game between Calgary and Toronto. There would be a week or so of celebration, much drinking, much spending, much clowning, and, I suppose, great quantities of aspirin.

How starved our people are for what they think is happiness! They will go anywhere, suffer any inconvenience, spend any amount of money, endure any miseries or privations, to attain it. Haven't you read about baseball fans who stay up all night, standing, sitting on rugs or stools they have brought with them or camping on the sidewalks to be sure of getting tickets for the world series?

Haven't you heard about men and women who spent their rent money for a seat at a "battle of the century" prizefight?

Again, one of my desert windows opened with a bang and I saw a long parade of pilgrims at the shrine of Our Lady of Lourdes. Each person had a lighted candle in one hand and many carried a rosary in the other. They were singing "Ave, Ave, Ave Maria" as they slowly walked through the grounds. It was night and I couldn't see any face clearly. There were no bands, no music except the voices of the people, no festooned floats, no cars of any kind, no rhythmic lifting of young knees.

Nobody waved. Nobody nodded. Nobody shouted. Nobody held up a bottle or a flask to show what a wonderful time he was having. Yet there was excitement in that solemn parade, more than there was in the parade through Vancouver's noisy avenue. And there was something extremely happy there. It was extremely happy because it was holy. It was a happiness that would last not for just an hour or a day or a week. It was a happiness that would live, though the whole world died!

It was there, in Lourdes, that I learned one can be truly happy only in a holy atmosphere.

There was no "million dollar gate" at Lourdes. No sports events. No theatrical attraction. No musical "must." There was only the statue of Our Blessed Lady and the fame of the many miracles God has wrought there. Yet perhaps Lourdes draws more visitors than all the sports areas and stadia and all the opera centers and all the art museums tourists love.

Many of its pilgrims are in great pain when they arrive. They pray for a miracle. The blind want to see again. The deaf want to hear. The lame want to run, to dance, to march in a big parade. The cripples want to be athletes. The dying want to live.

Some are cured. Most are not. Still, even those suffering the most pain find joy, a permanent joy. They become resigned to bear the cross the Lord has given them. They pray for miracles for others. Who can be happier than they are?

They come from every part of the world. They seek health, believing health is happiness. They discover holiness, and healed or not, they find that holiness provides true health, true joy.

Suddenly, right in the middle of the mirage, two shrill women began washing a dirty shirt. You just can't trust some mirages! On Sunday afternoon, before the Grey Cup game began, I was asked to say a few words at our weekly Pentecostal prayer meeting. I spoke about the human need for happiness and lasting peace; and about the devil who tries to give us hell.

I spoke of wars, massacres by starvation and by plague, the growing apathy toward religion in Canada and the United States. I spoke of the world's sore need for saints.

We went back to our easy chairs late that afternoon, Father Cal and I, and turned on the mirage. It was raining in Vancouver. The players splashed and skidded to their heart's content; and thousands of soppy fans cheered and screamed and waved from under their umbrellas or their twenty-gallon hats. The game ended—in champagne or chagrin, according to which team you bet on.

The mirage vanished and my desert was filled once more with peace and love.

On Monday morning, Thurston Smith, my faithful driver, drove me and my seeing-eye nurse to Toronto where I had another appointment with Dr. Callahan. Marian stayed overnight with a friend. Thurston and I found a hotel—and another mirage right there in our room! Billy Graham, one of my favorite preachers, was speaking to a great crowd somewhere in Texas. And he too was talking about the devil. He didn't like the demon any more than I did. He said so. Loud and clear! And he invited the crowd to accept Jesus and be happy.

You still alive and well, Billy?

Dr. Callahan was entranced with the work he had done on my eye. So were we. We stopped to buy three long-stemmed American Beauty roses. They were meant to celebrate a great day in my life—the day I first asked Catherine to marry me, the day she first said "No", in seven or eight different languages, thus spurring me on to a tremendous victory.

That was a gray day. It was in Chicago, November 30, 1941.

Three slender, long, fragrant roses would remind her of that moment thirty years ago. Three roses, three decades.

It had snowed during the night and the roads were slippery but passable. We picked up Margaret McHale before we started home and placed her carefully, gently, lovingly, in the back seat. She had been in a hospital and we were not quite sure she had entirely recovered from her operation. We handled her like a new-laid egg.

Thurston drove us to Peterboro without any trouble. At Peterboro Marian took the wheel and again we started home happy. When we were about sixty miles from Madonna House the car skidded on an icy stretch of concrete and went completely out of control.

It swerved to the right as though it wanted to jump into the snow-covered ditch. I couldn't help thinking, for a fraction of a moment, about Billy Graham's description of the Gadarene swine hurling themselves over a cliff into the sea because they were possessed by the demons Jesus had driven out of a madman.

Our car almost went off the road. Suddenly it veered to the left and flung itself and us toward a car coming around a bend in the road.

I wondered if the other driver could somehow manage to escape us. A collision seemed certain! Death was rushing towards us.

You've read stories about men facing death? All their past relives itself! They remember all their sins! They ask the good Lord to save them! They promise to be good if only they are spared!

Nonsense! There wasn't time to think of any sins. My life didn't regurgitate itself. I didn't remember anything--not even how happy we all had been a second before the car betrayed us. I felt I was going to be frightfully injured. I felt I might be killed. I felt we might all be killed.

But there wasn't time to be afraid. There wasn't time to make a "sincere act of contrition." There wasn't time to do anything for ourselves but get set for disaster. I set myself also—perhaps the only one in the car to do so—to get all the details so I could write the story for my paper. A newspaperman is always a newspaperman, it seems. Even when he's about to die he wants to write the story as accurately and as *pictorially* as he can.

We missed a nose-to-nose smashup by a few inches. Our car hit the other car at about the middle. The sound made by the impact disappointed me. I had wound myself up for the noise of a dynamite explosion. I have made louder noises with an air-filled paper bag.

I was thrown violently forward; yet I didn't go anywhere. I was too tightly strapped in the suicide seat, the one next to the driver. I saw the windshield turn white and send little wrinkles all over itself, the way a calm pool of water acts when rain begins to fall. I saw that our left front door had been torn off and that something awful had happened to Marian.

I saw our car wrench itself loose, swing around to the right, and prepare for a plunge into the ditch. It hesitated a moment on the edge of the road, then let go.

We bumped, bumped, bumped down the snow-covered incline, and stopped against a chicken wire fence. We sat there a long time, more or less silent. I looked over the bent wire fence into a stretch of ermine-wearing trees, their branches scratching the gray cheeks of the sky.

We were all alive! The devil had tried his best and failed. Had he tried to kill Billy Graham too?

Marian was uttering soft little prayers and we all knew she was suffering dreadfully. "Mary—Mary—Mary"—she was praying for us. I couldn't move around to look at her. Something was pinning me to my seat. It took me a long time to realize what it was. Then I unfastened the seat belt.

After a while we began to talk. Thurston was "all right." Margaret thought she might be hurt. She wasn't sure. She was still in shock. She had lost her eye-glasses. I had pain in my left side. I thought I had broken a rib or two. (Afterwards I discovered that one of my overcoat buttons had been broken, the one just below the seat belt lock.) It was the seat belt lock that furnished all my pain.

Within a very few minutes an Ontario Provincial Constable came slipping and sliding down to us out of his cruiser. He assured us that nobody in the other car had been hurt. He called an ambulance for us and he attended Marian as though she were a queen. His name is Carey. God bless him and all the other policemen in the world.

The ambulance took us to the Civic Hospital in Peterboro. Margaret and I were discharged the next day. Marian was the only one seriously hurt. Her pelvis had been cracked in three places. (Yet she was sent back to Madonna House before the week was ended, and her doctor said she would walk and run and dance again before the New Year starts.)

As I was being helped into the ambulance, Thurston handed me the roses I was carrying home to Catherine. Three long-stemmed American Beauties. Our three vows: Poverty, chastity, and obedience! Catherine and I made those vows long before I thought of becoming a priest.

"Keep them for her," I told Thurston.

A young and very pretty nurse brought them to me as I lay in the emergency ward. They were in a shallow bowl.

"They had your name on them, Father," the nurse said, "so they must be yours. But who could be sending you flowers so soon?" I was about to deny they were mine but the fragrance assured me. Yes, they were mine indeed, but the nice little nurse had cut their lovely long stems short so they could fit her bowl.

Catherine arrived at the hospital a few hours after Thurston phoned her.

"Who gave you the roses?" she asked.

Do you think she cared about the amputation of their stems?

We drove home slowly the next day, December 1st, and I concelebrated in a mass of thanksgiving.

Father Briere arranged an altar at the side of my bed—right here in this desert cell—and I lay back on a pile of pillows. Catherine was there and Thurston and others of the staff and, after the consecration and my communion, I had the joy of putting first the body of Christ into Catherine's hand; and then the chalice that contained Christ's blood!

And, speaking of pilgrimages and processions and parades, a solemn, magnificent, and most holy march began within me. Christ in his glorified body led the way with Our Lady at his side and millions of saints and angels behind him, singing and swinging censors full of the richest incense. And all my people living and dead were in line and all the people for whom I pray so often.

The desert is the perfect place for a parade.

Why don't we who hunger so terribly for happiness, so terribly neglect Almighty God, the source of happiness?

God made us to be happy here and hereafter. Let's be happy always.

15

HAPPY BIRTHDAY, LORD JESUS!

If you should hear that I am giving icebergs to everybody for Christmas, pay no attention. The story has very little truth in it. How could I get an iceberg—one iceberg—into my desert? How could I get several hundreds, one for each of my friends and two for Catherine? And what would Catherine do with them? Use them for earrings?

Christmas as everybody knows is a time for the silly and the sublime. It is a time for love and love embraces all silly and sublime things and thoughts and themes. But icebergs for Christmas? Why? God will provide plenty of ice on the roads and millions of scintillating iridescent icicles to hang from the eaves of our roofs—like so many Christmas stockings.

We spend plenty of time here in Madonna House on the silly and the sublime, on all things that give joy to people. Since we are all poor, we are all beggars. We do not buy presents for one another. We make them. Sometimes with great skill, sometimes with very little skill. But always with patience and work and love.

The more you love God, the more you love your neighbor. The more you love your neighbor, the more you love God. We show our love for God by making something pretty or lovely or exquisitely beautiful, or crazy and ridiculous and absurd, and giving it to those we love with the love of God stamped into every part of it.

Some work with paper, papier-mache, linen, metal, wood, plastics, paints, water colors, crayons, pottery, candles, clay, dired flowers or anything handy. Some make us songs. Some create skits. Some write idiotic drivel (like me). Some make funny jewelry or carve comic figures for their friends, some draw cartoons.

Today it is raining and sleeting; therefore I cannot open my windows and let you see Madonna House getting ready for the day of all celestial days. You would look at girls doing mysterious and magnificent things in the kitchen.

The smell of baking cookies and pies! The blessed fragrance of spices! And all the other exciting aromas—too bad we have to keep the windows closed!

Another window would show you girls making gifts, girls packaging gifts, girls sorting gifts, girls hurrying to and fro with multi-colored papers and gold and silver cords and bags full of mistletoe and holly (mostly imitations), and girls emptying great cardboard cartons of their treasures so that other girls can sort them and mark them so they will go where Heaven wants them to go.

Preparations for Christmas begin in Madonna House on December 26th and last until midnight December 24th and 25th the following year.

Thousands of gifts are distributed at Christmas and through the year; clothing, furniture, costume jewelry. Gadgets and gimmicks. Dolls and toys. Balls and bats and gloves and hockey sticks. Candies of all kinds. Hankies and handbags. Musical instruments. Books. And home-made bread and buns and mince-meat pies, and the Lord only knows what else. It's all distributed in time for the holy child to enjoy it.

On Christmas Eve as the hour of glory approaches, in the Spanish tradition of the Posadas, groups of singers greeted the weary Joseph and Mary with warning cries: "Be off with you, you beggars. There's no room for you here."

But this is hushed and Father Cal, our chaplain, appears with the new-born infant in his arms and we accompany him to the chapel.

Usually many priests concelebrate the midnight mass, and the Madonna House choir always tries to outdo the angels who sang to the shepherds so many years ago. And each priest says three masses during the day.

My masses, my Christmas present to Madonna House and to all the world, will be said with great joy and will be offered for the sick and the dying, for all the unfortunate and poor, all the humiliated and degraded and abused, all prisoners, all travellers, all the hopeless and despairing, all those contemplating a better birthplace than that dirty old hole!

Lift the chalice with me. And drink from it. It will hold enough treasure to buy peace on earth and good will to men. It will shed a light powerful enough to guide even the blind to safety. And it will fill you all with illimitable love.

Gather under the window and sing "Happy birthday Lord Jesus; happy birthday to you."

He loved the wise men. He'll love you.

16

THE HOUSE OF ALMA

'From my heart has sprung
A beautiful song.
It is my whole life
I have given
To the king.'

Our Madonna House choir was singing in the new chapel we built on Hermit Island. It was almost time for midnight mass. It was Christmas Eve, but this particular song had nothing to do with rubric or ritual. It is a song we sing when the staff workers take their promises of poverty, chastity, and obedience; or when one of them is sent from Combermere to one of our missions; or when one of them has died.

This song was for Alma Beauchamp. And, as the words indicate, it was about her. Years ago she gave up her life to the king and yesterday he had accepted it.

I was sitting in a chair near the altar waiting for mass to begin; and I was filled with many wonders. It was a wonder that we had a chapel here in the thickness of the "back bush," where no man had ever built anything before—except perhaps a wigwam made of the branches of virgin pines. It was a wonder that it should look so little and be so big. It was a wonder that it should be so beautiful and comfortable and so complete! And it was a wonder that it had been sufficiently finished at this particular time—not only for midnight mass but also for Alma's funeral.

Waiting there in my chair beside the altar and listening to the exultant voices of the singers, one of my desert windows opened and I saw myself guiding two Canadian priests about the little towns of Galilee a week or so before my ordination. I took them first to a funeral mass. They were somewhat shocked to hear the priests on the altar and the men in the congregation singing "Alleluia, Alleluia, Alleluia!"

I had to explain to them that this was really part of the Byzantine liturgy. Exultation! Because a soul had found its home, its Lord, its eternal joy. Alleluia, alleluia, alleluia. I took them next to a wedding ceremony. In that liturgy there were no "alleluias" sung, only "kyrie eleisons."

Alma had come home to us from the hospital in Ottawa. She had told the doctors she would like to be "home for Christmas," so they let her come. Most of us were at dinner when we heard that she was dying. We went immediately to the chapel over the dining-room—our first little chapel. And we were praying for her when someone rushed in saying "Alleluia, she is with the Lord."

Alma, I thought, could be compared to this chapel. She too was a house of God. She was like the temple built by Solomon; but undoubtedly much more attractive to the Lord. Solomon had built his structure out of the costliest materials and he had covered everything with solid gold. But he had employed thousands and thousands of slaves in the work and he had made a temple not to God but to himself—or so it seems to me.

David had wanted to build the structure, but was not permitted to do so. "I live in a cedar palace," he explained to Nathan, "while the ark of the covenant abides in a tent."

Nathan talked to the Lord. And the Lord said to him: "Who is David to make a house for me?" He explained that it was he who had made a house for David, a house that would exist so long as the world existed. David was a house of the Lord. So was Alma.

There was nothing ornate in Alma's house, nothing pretentious, nothing expensive and gaudy. It has been built as this chapel was built—by patience and faith and love and the graces showered on the Madonna House Apostolate by Our Lady, the virgin mother of Almighty God.

The choir sang about Alma and about the baby born in a stable in a cave in the Bethlehem hills and laid in a manger. And they sang about his death and resurrection. And they sang about his mercy and his love.

And we went back to Madonna House and celebrated Christmas; and returned to the chapel of Our Lady of the Woods for the funeral mass on Monday morning.

I was sitting again in the chair beside the altar when they brought the body in. First they set up two "wooden horses," and placed a flat board across it—a board big enough and strong enough to support a coffin. Someone covered this with a white cloth. Someone lovingly smoothed all the wrinkles out of the linen, touching it lightly and reverently, as though it belonged to the altar.

Then they brought the coffin in and set it gently down. Gently, so gently, that a priest quite close to me could not help shedding a scalding, shining tear. Then Catherine placed an ikon on the casket, as Alma had asked her to do. An ikon of Our Lady and the Child. Our Lady in a beautiful blue robe.

It was a beautiful coffin. It was plain and simple, an

ordinary pine box with handles for the pallbearers. It had been built as the chapel was built and by some of the people who helped to build it—Father Paul Bechard, Father Tom Zoeller, and Bill Jakali, the chapel's architect.

It was a little chapel in itself. Had Alma moved from a chapel made of flesh into one made of pine? Not really. Alma had gone from a house of God straight into the arms of God and he had a palace waiting for her.

The chapel began to fill. Some people had come from great distances, but most of them were our neighbors. Alma drew many people to her, though it might be only in a continuous correspondence. People wrote her about their problems, their troubles, their hopes, their ambitions, their failings, and their faults. She found time to answer them. God gave her the time and the desire and the strength. She lived close to him, day and night. She ate his body and drank his blood every morning. Frequently priests said mass beside her bed—at home or in the hospital—and frequently they gave her the sacrament of the sick.

She knew that in the chalice of every priest saying mass there is enough blood to save the whole world and give joy and peace and love to every living soul. She profited greatly through that knowledge.

She knew also that most men spurn the blood of Christ and glut themselves on the blood of their brothers. She prayed for them. She offered her sufferings for them—and for all the needy and all the poor and all the children of God who do not know they have a Father.

Our Bishop, the Most Reverend Joseph Windle, surrounded by sixteen priests, presided at the mass. Father Briere, Alma's spiritual director for many years, said a very few words—and those were excerpts from her own diary. I remember only one, "Death is not separation; it is union with God."

His talk was like the coffin—plain, simple, beautiful, warming.

The choir sang the requiem music; but alleluias crept into their voices.

After the mass we followed the body to the parish graveyard; and my desert windows opened on the way.

There were only three of us in Madonna House, Catherine, Grace Flewelling, and I. It was bitter cold walking through the arcade of tall pines to the little white church down the road and all the way we smelled the joyous turpentine odor of the trees. Only the three of us and only a six-room cottage!

Now, there were many in line; the way was long—it gets longer every year—and there was no noticeable aroma in the trees. Nor were there many trees left standing on the road and Alma would rest beside Grace Flewelling and wait for company to come.

A few days ago the pines, especially those that surround the chapel in the woods, were white hoods like some ancient order of monks—and white surplices and long white stoles. Today they were free of snow. They stood rejoicing as we passed beneath them. We, who have given our whole lives to the king. But what is that, compared to what he has given us? Each one of us, like Alma, is a house of the Lord, built by the Lord—with very little cooperation.

And each of us someday will move from that house into a mansion in the sky with the help of the Lord and the graces given us by his Mother.

Alma's funeral today; ours tomorrow. Hosanna in the highest. Alleluia, Alleluia, Alleluia.

17

STANDS TO REASON

A fat little man hurried by my window—the one that looks on Galilee and Judea. He was holding his many colored robes above his knees, exposing his overstuffed hairy legs and sandaled feet. He seemed to be running in fear of his life. A great crowd of people followed him. But the people, it became evident, were not chasing the little man. They were not even aware of him. They clustered about another man. They were excited, reverent, joyful. They were escorting Jesus.

So the man who had fled was Zachaeus, the principal tax collector of the area! And he was going to climb a tree so that he could have a real good look at Jesus.

The gospel of the day had turned from so much print into something like a moving picture in the days before the pictures learned to speak.

Zachaeus didn't know he had no need to hurry, had no need to climb a tree. The moment he decided to find Jesus, Jesus found him and was waiting to embrace him. It is thus with every man who seeks him.

It was good to watch Zachaeus climb down from the tree, tearing his rich attire and laughing at it; and to watch him lead the master so humbly into his pretentious home.

I seemed to hear voices. Silent but penetrating. "What kind of man is this who claims to be the son of God yet singles out a public sinner to give him such a great honor? Well, Zachaeus is a sinner, but he is also filthy rich. He pretends to love the poor, but it stands to reason he prefers the rich and mighty."

Men trying to understand the ways of God! Poor, imperfect, human minds daring to compete with the infinite wisdom of their Creator!

I began to meditate on the fatal difference between reason, however brilliant and logical it may be, and faith.

God endowed man with reason, one of his greatest gifts. Man used it to kill off all his enemies, animal and human, and to conquer the earth and fill it with music and beauty and wonders of all kinds. He used it to tame the stars and make a gold club—and a parking place—of the moon. He used it to wrap the world with wires, to shrink the oceans, and to construct a million pathways through the skies.

He also used it to improve the destructiveness of war and massacre and common murder, and to tackle the population question in a scientific manner. It is time, human reason argues, that God stay out of the population picture. He made far too many people; and if he isn't checked he will make too many more. He needs Yankee know-how, modern techniques, "expertise." So the "big brains" must take over.

Reason is indeed a sovereign gift of heaven; but how many people know how to use it? Some reason themselves into power and fame and tax-free bags of money; others into kidnapping, hijacking, bigamy, suicide or murder; and still others into taking vows of of lifelong poverty, obedience and chastity.

Reason is as fickle as the weather. It differs in everyone, in every clime, in every state and nation. It has its highs and lows, its crazy eddies, its shifting winds. And it is always "subject to change." Like the weather.

The scene began to fade. I was about to close the window when I happened to see three crosses pasted on the pale gray sky over Calvary.

I looked at one of the thieves who was crucified with Jesus. He too was "up a tree," but not exactly as Zachaeus was. He was young and tough and bitter. And he hated and despised Jesus even more, it seemed, than he hated the crowds below who came here to watch him die.

This showed in the way he looked at the man beside him. I couldn't hear anything he said but I could understand it. "So you are God, are you? And you are also the king of the Jews! Why did you let them crown you with that silly crown? Don't you know that one of the thorns is sticking in your eye? You're a phony. You're worse than either of us two. We never claimed to be anything but sinners. You—you blasphemer!"

But suddenly, for no apparent reason—perhaps some look in the forgiving eyes of Jesus—reason gave way to faith. And he cried out his belief in God and his hope of salvation. "Remember me, Lord, when you come into your kingdom."

Jesus didn't tell him to come down from the tree, but he did invite him to a banquet that night in Paradise.

One moment reason ruled this suffering wretch and poisoned him with hate. The next moment a miraculous faith made him the first saint to enter heaven.

The shifting light caught the face of the other thief for a few seconds and revealed his thoughts also. "Hey you, you messiah, if you are really the messiah—you're wasting your time praying for those stinking slobs below. Are you trying to weasel your way off the wood by softening them? No dice.

Look at them. Worse than wolves. Your bitterest enemies!
They enjoy your suffering. They feel big. If you are
anything like you say you are, get off that cross. Save
yourself. And us! Rain fire down on the heads of that
howling mob and damn them all to hell! The real God
smashed things when he got mad. He burned two big cities.
He drowned a whole army in the Red Sea. Hey, he even
turned a woman into salt when she merely provoked him! If
you were really God, you wouldn't just stay there and bleed
to death praying for them. Stands to reason."

He heard his friend ask for mercy and remembrance.
And he writhed with anger. "He's gone soft," he shouted.
"You made him go soft. That's what you do to men. A man
should be hard. He should stay hard like me. Who needs a
God that'll soften him—especially a fake God? You're bad
luck, messiah, and you're a menace to guys that won't be
tamed."

The hard thief held onto his reason, such as it was, and
was cast into hell. No? Maybe not. Yet it stands to reason,
doesn't it?

A gentle breeze blew in through the window. The three
crosses vanished, like a mirage in the desert of the years.

But the crowd remained. No. It was a different crowd, in
a different place.

This must have been before the crucifixion, for Jesus was
there, his back turned to me, and he was talking about his
body and his blood.

I was looking into the faces of a few men who stood
before him. They stepped back abruptly, sick with fear and
horror. One would have thought the Lord was handing
them a poisonous and loathsome viper.

Again I could hear silent voices:

"Eat his flesh; drink his blood? What are we? Cannibals? Drink his blood! What son of Abraham drinks blood? The soul of the animal is in the blood. Must we eat him raw or kill and cook him first? What would Moses say about eating the flesh of any man, especially one who claims to be divine? He is making fools of us.

He tells us he is God, then says we must eat him, dead or alive, to have life in us! What mortal would dare eat the flesh of God—if God indeed had flesh? What fool would dare to drink his blood?"

Those men left the crowd to walk with him no more. And others followed. Many others. And the Lord was alone with his apostles who had not understood a word he said, but who had believed in him. Jesus could easily have explained his beautiful mystery; but he preferred to do so at the right time and only to those who had kept faith in him.

The window closed gently and I found myself near the end of the divine liturgy. I was about to consume what was left on the paten and in the chalice after holy communion. His flesh was meat indeed and his blood was drink indeed. And I was the most fortunate of men because it was mine to have and to hold.

Suppose I had been standing under that center cross with his mother and John and Mary Magdalen and the others, would I have dared to lift myself high enough to sip the last drops from the chalice made in his heart by the Roman lance? Probably not.

But I rejoiced that I could drink from the golden lip of my chalice, not the body and blood of the dead and defeated God, but that of his triumphant and glorious risen self.

I closed the window gently and tried to open its neighbor, the one that faces heaven. But as usual I couldn't budge it.

A silent voice behind me was repeating words from the gospel I had read during the liturgy: "I must dine with you today. Today salvation has come to your house."

The marvel is that the words were spoken not to Zachaeus nor the good thief on the cross. They were intended only for me!

I believe that. And I believe it was the Lord himself who spoke.

I believe Lord, help thou my unbelief!

18

THE LORD'S PARADE

On the 17th of May, 1972, Madonna House celebrated the silver anniversary of its founding. Together, we are beginning to realize what an amazing twenty-five years we have spent in this Canadian back-bush, this wilderness, this hidden community, this thriving Catholic mecca.

All these years we have fattened on the daily manna of the Lord. All these years we have witnessed daily miracles and took them for granted as something we had a right to expect. All these years we have walked on the water of God's loving providence; nonchalant, untroubled, unworried, not even thinking we were doing anything impossible or unusual in any way. Sometimes the winds were chill and the waves were high but we never even wet our feet.

Is it odd that a man who lives in a desert should take a daily stroll on the water? Then let it continue to be odd.

Is it odd that there should be a garden in that desert? And is it odd that both garden and desert are portable?

It is odder still that for twenty-five years I have neither noticed nor appreciated its oddity.

I spent some of the winter in our desert-garden in Winslow, Arizona. (The doctors and nurses who rule my life and run my earthly pilgrimage want me to walk every day; but it is impossible to walk in six feet of snow and ice.) In Arizona the sun shines every day. And if there is snow it lasts but an hour.

I was in Arizona admiring the flowers in my garden and

enjoying the cloister of my desert when I was summoned home to Canada. I must be present at the day of the silver jubilee. So I set out taking half the garden with me, three staff workers of Madonna House.

What shall I liken them to? Roses? Roses are too proud, too regal. Lilies? Never! Lilies are posers. And they are only for the dead—or for plaster saints.

We have no standardized blossoms in our garden of souls. Each is different from all the others. Some are female. Some are males. We are women, lay men and priests—ordinary people who do ordinary tasks, monotonous daily chores, jobs that pay not even a nickel a year. We have no ambition to do anything else. We are ordinary but unusual. We try to obey the will of God, knowing that God wishes only the best for each of us. We realize that he wants us all to be happy; and that we can be happy only in doing what he wants, not what we want.

The honey bees of holiness pollinate the flowers bringing them to maturity, to beauty and to fragrance, and giving them seeds with which they can spread beauty and peace and love throughout the world.

My travelling companions were different species of marigolds or maybe snapdragons; humble flowers that hide in the shade of hollyhocks, sunflowers, poppies, mums or daisies. They may be meek and little but they have a zip and a snap to them. And what a spicy aroma!

They shared a supreme moment with me on the trip. The engineer stopped suddenly—maybe to spit his cud onto the tracks. We looked out the window and saw white rings of clouds, hovering like halos over the far purple mountains, and the last rays of the sun bringing glory down on white peaks nearby. The cars paused long enough to let the passengers say a prayer of thanks, then jolted on with a loud amen.

There were no purple mountains in the backyard of Madonna House, Combermere, when we arrived. But from its three rear doors groups of men and women rushed to welcome us home—and their halos were in their eyes.

Eye speaks to eye in this garden and heart to heart; and sometimes lip brushes lip in the happiness of reunion. (And God takes fresh delight in his children, the children of Mary.)

It was hot and dry when we left Arizona. It was actually summer and we had been looking forward to the happiness of seeing, smelling, and tasting the dawn of a Canadian spring. I expected to see robins and red-winged blackbirds and maybe the old blue crane that loves our Madawaska marsh. I expected to see trees still wet with their first coats of pale green paint, pulling themselves high up from their roots so that they could brush their top branches against the blue of the sky and stain it.

I hoped to see froglets playing leap-frog in the new garden grass; and troops of little turtles scrambling from their broken (and useless) eggs across the yellow sands to the shining azure river. But there was neither bird nor bud, frog nor turtle, and all the trees were dead except the cedars and the spruces and the firs and the pines.

There was ice in the river, and great patches of snow lay in the bleachers of the hills and fields and in the dark shadows of the woods. The snow was gray with age and grime, but it was covered with an intricate lace made by the needles of the rain and the sun and the wind. The sun was skulking behind gray clouds. I couldn't see him but I could hear him. He was in his fiery pulpit repeating his daily sermon. "Death today, tomorrow resurrection."

No signs of spring? What about that girl with a bucket in either hand? One bucket was yellow and the other bright red and each was more than half filled with sap.

"The boys are milking the maples," she said. "We're going to have plenty of maple syrup. I'm burping the birches for wine. Did you know it takes eighty gallons of sap to make one gallon of birch wine and only forty gallons to make one gallon of maple syrup? Men have all the luck. Well, welcome home."

"Where did you get the bright new pails?" I asked.

"Donation," she said. (I knew she was going to say it. When we need anything the Lord listens.) "Somebody sent us a thousand of them. Maybe twelve hundred. Anyway a lot of them."

The boys had put 160 taps in 140 maple trees and they said the sap was running "fast and full." "Best job I ever had," one of them said; "but I wish we had had some high boots. Walking in deep snow around all those trees half a day or longer is a lot of fun, but it's hard work carrying the sap away, especially when you stumble or the snow gets too deep. You lift the pails high and if you joggle them even a little, the sap runs down your arms and covers your armpits with ice."

The Lord's love pours itself out to us even from the trees. Taste and see that the Lord is sweet. Let the Madawaska clap its hands and all the foothills of the Laurentians shout for joy.

I was about to unroll my desert and enter into its

enriching silence when a servant came to fetch me to a fashion show. Gisele, who lives on Hermit Island in the desert built of logs, had committed a miracle with scraps of black cloth taken from the habits of nuns and pieces of silk and satin linings from clerical vestments. Somehow, she had turned them into "the most stunning dresses you ever saw."

The show was held in St. Raphael's, our spacious arts and crafts pavilion across the road. I watched it for awhile remembering fashion shows I had seen as a newspaperman in Chicago, Hollywood, New York, and several other capitals of style. And I listened, or half listened, to someone explaining what it was all about. But I was distracted.

One of my magic windows had slammed open and I was reliving another kind of show. This happened in our basement years and years ago when we had only a few clothes to give away and hardly any place to store them. It happened when our unmapped five acres of sand seemed farther than thirteen miles from the nearest railroad station. When we had no bus service, and all the roads were impassable most of the time. Naturally we had only a few donations. What a difference the long years make!

As I was going down the steps from the kitchen to throw a log or two into the furnace I could see there was a woman with Catherine. Her back was turned but I knew she was a neighbor. And she was crying. Catherine had given her two colorful dresses and she was trying to say thanks. "Two. Two boughten dresses! I ain't had a boughten dress since I was married. Now I got two of them. Just like that!"

After she was gone Catherine looked at the pile of clothing in the corner near the wash tubs and the crazy gasoline-driven pump which never worked until I cursed it or Catherine asked the help of Our Lady of Combermere.

"Some day," she said, "I am going to have a real clothing room, a big one. And some day I'm going to teach the women of Combermere to make clothes for themselves and their children. Why they don't all go crazy in the winter I don't know. Their husbands and eldest sons are out in the bush logging. There's nothing else for the men to do. They won't be back until the snow melts. All the wives do is tend the house, get the meals, and take care of the children. They don't go visiting. They live too far apart and the snow is too deep. If they had something interesting to do in their long idle hours like sewing or knitting or making things they could sell to tourists in the summer and fall, they wouldn't mind being shut up so many months."

Since that day many local women have learned the art of dressmaking. And, if you will look around you will see, right here in this vicinity, some of the best-dressed women in the world!

I watched the show and the parade of the models with awe and wonder. Talents bloom in this place as well as virtues. I never saw more alluring feminine duds anywhere—not even in the women's magazines.

I got one of the girls to describe them for me, thinking that possibly somebody else might be as interested as I was.

All the time I was watching and listening and sipping tea, some of our girls were conspiring behind my back. I had no inkling of it until the eve of our celebration.

The chapel of Our Lady of the Woods, an exquisite gem of architecture designed by Bill Jakali, was ready and waiting. The ikons sent to us from Athens by our friend,

Archbishop Joseph Raya of the See of Galilee, had been put in their proper places. Our bishop had promised to say the mass. The choir knew exactly what to sing. Hundreds of people had promised to come and all preparations had been made for their arrival. A ton or two of food had been prepared.

And only then I learned that some of the women who made the dresses had made a set of golden Eastern-rite vestments for me! I am the best dressed priest in North America!

We walk indeed on the waters of God's Providence. And if a big wave splashes us, it splashes us with blessings—even with cloth of gold!

19

A PROMISE FULFILLED

A long time ago some oofty-goofty child of a stupid dromedary buried a treasure in the sands of my desert. He went away forgetting what he had done and where he had done it. He didn't realize it was a treasure more sublime and more enduring and a thousand times more to be desired than gold, the frankincense and the myrrh the Magi brought to the stable of a new-born king.

The other day, through one of those accidents God arranges to help idiots and authors and editors and other unfortunates, he let me find it! And great was the joy in my oasis!

The same stupy-dupy had lost my Book of the Gospels. A Byzantine priest must have this on the altar when he sings the divine liturgy. This one was conspicuous by its beauty. The Madonna House staff workers in Winslow, Arizona, had covered it with a tailor-made red velvet coat and the staff workers of Madonna House in Combermere had added a bright gold braid to it. No one could possibly have mislaid that gorgeous living book except the oaf who forgot where he hid the treasure.

I searched among the living books in every library in the house, and there are quite a few. It was not there. I looked at the dead and dying volumes. There was no lovely red velvet in their neat, orderly rows of paper shrouds and cloth or leather mummy cases. I even visited the library in the kitchen. The cookbooks all stood erect, prim and solemn like gravestones with aprons, marking the remains of some old gravies. I returned to my room and chose one of the living books that stand between the polished slabs of petrified wood—wood that died a billion years ago or more, yet still has life enough to live into eternity.

And there was the unexpected cache of heavenly riches. It was marked only by a paper angel. Not a guardian angel evidently, nor yet a fallen angel despite the fact that she had slipped, head downward, between two pages as comfortably as if they had been made of Irish linen—and had slept on her pretty head for lo these many years!

She was still asleep when she fell through my excited fingers into the waste basket at my feet, her head pillowed on a dead cigarette butt.

I was stooping to pick her up when I saw the glint of the treasure—the gift the new born king had meant for the Magi, the wise men who had travelled so far to find him.

"I give you my word; there is no one who gives up home, brothers or sisters, mother or father, children or property, for me and for the Gospel, who will not receive in the present age a hundred times as many homes, brothers, sisters, mothers, children and property, and persecutions beside—and in the age to come, eternal life."

The promise of the Lord!

Catherine and I had left all things for Christ. For him and for his Gospel. So had many others, young men and women who had come to Madonna House. We had not worked for any reward. We had not thought of a reward. We worked for God, one might say, reverently—"just for the hell of it!"

And all the time that hidden treasure grew and grew!

We hadn't asked for any pay. But now we could prove

that we had been paid more than a hundred times the ordinary wages.

We could prove it to all the people who come here—and they come from all over the world and they come in the thousands; we could say, "Look around you and see how the Lord has blessed us."

We have hayfields, meadows, farms and woodlands, a collection of houses and barns and chapels, and a four-car garage that never housed a single one of our machines. It is used only to store the clothing and other gifts coming to us like tides at the flood that ebb away from us to poor families all around us or dribble somehow into our gift shop. God sends us new supplies every day or so—sometimes in trucks that travel hundreds of miles; vehicles tough enough and big enough to frighten the wits out of a freight car.

A promise filled and flowing over! Gifts of all kinds come to us daily, some in long caravans of sublime and beautiful fancies and ideas. The very sands of my desert are saturated with these blessings.

Let me tell you of a thought that came to me on the feast of Saint Mary Magdalen. That day I noticed something extra special about the wine, something so wonderful it still exalts me!

Early in my priesthood I had experienced wonderful things connected with the wine I consecrated and thus changed, with the help of the Lord, into the blood of Christ. It tasted like good wine, very good wine. Nothing more. Yet when I drained the chalice after giving communion to my little flock, the wine I poured into it to cleanse my fingers—the same wine I had enjoyed a few minutes before, poured from the came cruet—that wine tasted almost sour!

I was skeptical at first. I felt I was simply imagining a

difference. Wine was wine, especially out of the same container. But it was possible, I admitted, that ordinary wine, blessed and consecrated, could be both mystically and physically changed—as the water was changed into wine at the marriage feast in Cana of Galilee.

God was letting me taste the wine that had been kept to the last—the wine of divine vintage!

It was on the feast of the beautiful Magdalen, July 22nd, while I concelebrated with other Madonna House priests in the Roman-rite mass, that I became aware of another miracle. Well, maybe not a miracle. Maybe only a supreme gift wafted down from heaven.

I sipped the divine and human blood of the Lord, then turned to give his body to several dozen men and women and two little girls. The celebrant gave each communicant a sip from the chalice and then handed the golden cup to me.

I drank a little of its contents—and tasted heaven!

This time there was no imagination. The wine was glorified!

It was of course, impossible. How could anything divine be so divinely bettered?

It was also impossible that I could be mistaken about the taste. There was a tremendous difference between the first and the second sips. That change was not in me. It was in the precious blood itself!

I am sure nobody alive, no matter how wise he might be in the ways of God, could tell me what had happened.

Back in my room I tried to open all my desert windows at the same time to let in light, understanding, and knowledge; and to let out all the wonder and excitement and ecstasy and thanksgiving and love that almost suffocated me. "Blow in, Wind of the Holy Ghost."

The only window that worked was the one that looks on Calvary and Galilee and all the places touched by the holy feet of Christ. I saw nothing at all for a minute or so. Then I made out the figure of a woman crouched below a cross. Somebody was holding a smoky torch because the day was dark. In its light I could see the woman's red hair shining, and I could just barely see a man's feet, one nailed above the other. Presently the silent voice God lets me hear so often began its explanation.

"The chalice, when it was given you the second time, contained not only the Blood of Jesus Christ, but many other precious things. It held the love of the prodigal son for his father and the father's love for his son. It held their love of God and God's love for them. It held the tears and the love of Mary Magdalen, and Christ's joy at her tears and his great love for her and for all repentant sinners. It held the love of all those people who drank from it after you did, all their prayers, their hopes, their loneliness, their weaknesses and their strengths; all they have given to Jesus and all he has given to them. It held the happiness heaven knows at the return of a sinner to the fold—and the happiness that a sinner feels in the shepherd's caressing hands. The wine wasn't changed but it had taken on a human flavor; and it was indeed a taste of heaven!"

Nobody keeps his promises as the Lord does. He not only pours material gifts upon us, he also showers manna in the desert of our minds.

Incidentally, the Book of Gospels, in its lovely red jacket, lay all the time I was searching for it under a newspaper on my desk. Mr. Oofty-Goofty had thrown the paper there and forgotten to remove it.

20

NUNS, NUNS, NUNS

Not too many years ago an old nun crippled with arthritis lay, seemingly abandoned, in a dingy ward in a dingy general hospital in Brooklyn. All the nurses and all the other patients in the ward were sure she was insane for all she ever said was, "policemen, policemen, policemen," or maybe "railroad men, railroad men, railroad men—street walkers, street walkers, street walkers." It could also be "taxi drivers, taxi drivers, taxi drivers"—or even "politicians, politicians, politicians."

When a nurse finally asked her what she was mumbling about she answered, "I'm trying to pray for everybody in the world. The only way I can do that is to mention people aloud. If I don't, I go to sleep. So I pray aloud, "waiters, waiters, waiters."

The other morning as I said the divine liturgy in my oasis, I became aware that something was missing in our prayers.

A priest of the Melkite-rite prays for peace in the world, for favorable weather, for abundance of the fruits of the earth, for the sick, the suffering, the prisoners, the travellers by sea, air, and land; "for our deliverance from all affliction, wrath, danger and need," for His Holiness, Pope Paul, for the bishop who ordained him, for the bishop of the diocese, for the reverend clergy, for the deacons, "for our public servants, for the government, and all those who protect us," and for our brothers and sisters who have been laid to holy rest."

The book was compiled by holy men who seemed to regard every woman as another Eve—and therefore another evil. But once she was buried it was all right to pray for her. (Dead men tell no tales; dead women tempt no males.) The young man trained for the priesthood could marry when he was a deacon—if he wished to. Once he was ordained a priest however, he was supposed to forget about women; while he was saying the divine liturgy anyway. And take it or leave it, nuns—even the holiest of them—were women. Maybe that's why the nuns were never publicly prayed for; maybe there was some other reason. Maybe there was no reason at all. It was the men who went to church in those days. The women stayed home so that they would have all the chores done and a delicious meal waiting for them when the men came home.

Maybe I have a soft spot in my spiny cactus heart for nuns—and for nun-like women. Maybe I haven't. But I decided to devote a lot of my time at the altar and in my desert cell to praying for nuns, nuns, nuns.

I was strengthened in this decision by the news that two of my favorite nuns had gone joyously to heaven.

A Madonna House priest wrote me about one of them.

"On Wednesday evening she asked for a candle to be placed in her room because our Lord was there with communion for her. After a few moments of quiet she said, "It's fine now. You can blow it out."

A nun wrote me about the second.

"She was happy to get your letter and wanted me to write to you for her but the divine thief came himself to take her home, to be with him, Mary, St. Joseph, and all her wonderful friends who have gone before her. She had been suffering much, she was so worried about the whole world, and about our nuns in secular dress. This is my home until I stop breathing. I hope someone will tell you if I go before you."

The world is full of hate and lust and greed and anger and fear. But the world is blessed with convents where nuns pray all day and all night for railroad conductors, policemen, taxi drivers, politicians, adulterers, murderers, you and me, and all the other sinners in the world.

There's no use trying to open the desert window that faces God and all his heavenly court. It sticks tighter and tighter at every attempt to look through it. So I go to another window and look on other nuns I love—many who are still living. I remember an old friend of my boyhood; Saint Juliana Falconieri. When she was dying she could not open her mouth wide enough to receive the host. She motioned the priest to place the wafer over her heart. The priest obliged her. The host immediately disappeared. I remember a nun who regarded herself as a total loss to her convent. Because she couldn't walk without awful pain she was put in the "altar bread" section of the convent. She made hosts all day long and stacked them. But she said a prayer with every host she made—a prayer for priests and for all who would receive her product from the hands of the priests.

There are nuns just like her in almost every convent. And there are many women in our Madonna House Apostolate who lead similar lives. Some of them make altar bread. Some work in the laundry or the kitchen or the gardens and fields or the office or the library. Some make bread. Some make candles. Some churn butter. Some paint pictures.

Some sort jewelry. Some scrub floors. The work is monotonous, unvarying, tedious. But to the women of Madonna House work is prayer. Sometimes the work is changed. Someone is appointed to one of our mission houses to teach catechism, to visit the poor and see what they need, to help people help themselves and others, and to do a thousand other things, unexciting things.

The average nun is as forgotten as the caterpillar in its warm cocoon. She is remembered only when she becomes a gorgeous butterfly and delights all heaven with her presence.

Most of us tend to classify nuns not as women at all but as females who "got religion" or as fanatics or as a nice and sweet and harmless sort of lunatic. But there is more "woman" in them than in any of your "libs" or your modern crusaders for sterilization or infanticide or those who think that "women's rights" will right all wrongs.

Once upon a time somewhere in Greece or Turkey or Lebanon or Israel or Jordan or France or Sweden—or someplace else—I was abruptly set down to dinner with a dozen nuns who could speak only French. We were strangers and we embarrassed each other since I had only a few French words to offer.

"No French?" one asked me. "No French at all?"

I recalled two words I had picked up somewhere. "Embrassez-moi," I didn't know exactly what it meant but I knew somehow that it was something pleasant.

The nuns laughed merrily. Then one rose and ran to me. She kissed me on the cheek. Like a good Christian I turned the other cheek. She kissed that too. Then all the rest of them followed her example. And immediately we were no longer strangers; we were a family in love with God and with one another.

Nuns, like the women of Madonna House, love God first, their neighbors second, and themselves last of all.

The nuns and the staff workers who have died are buried in my private—and portable—desert. They pray for me and I pray for them and for all nuns everywhere in heaven and on earth.

21

ENJOY GOD NOW

"June," Maid Marion said. "It's really June! And from what I've already seen I'd predict there will soon be millions and millions of wild strawberries running all over this place."

She happened to glance out of the north window of my room above the kitchen here in Madonna House—the room to which all the good smells come.

"All those blossoms," she exclaimed. "Aren't they lovely! Isn't God good!"

You go down on your hands and knees for the sweetness of God, I thought. And you stand up and reach out your hands to him or you climb to the very top of the tree for his gifts. You find him at all levels. You enjoy him as much in the September apple as you do in the wild June berry.

Let us enjoy him at every minute of the time allotted to us. Let's begin to enjoy him now. Right now. It may be too late tomorrow.

I must have spoken a word or two out loud for the girl gave me a peculiar look.

"Yes," she said. "Right now."

"Right now what?"

"Father Eddie, you are thinking again. I said I have come to take you for a ride. It's my day off. And Doreen's too. We want you to come right now."

Marian was my "seeing eye doll" during the time I spent in Toronto getting my right eye detached from its ever loving, every-clinging cataract. Doreen has come back to Madonna House after a long series of operations.

"Wonderful," I said. "Where shall we go?"

"How would you like to see the place where we're going to erect the archive building?"

A window opened in my portable desert—the window that's always loose, the one that flops open at every thought of the pronoun I; the window with the daffy view, the one that gazes grimly on my past.

Through the pane I saw a guest who was here some years ago. He was a goodlooking man named Goldberg or Sullivan or Kozlowski or something like that. And he wrote a very funny essay about Catherine, the B, the beehives and her arch hives.

I remember him perfectly but I couldn't recall his name or exactly what he had written.

That didn't matter for he had flattened my newspaperman's nose to a strange and exciting trail of thought.

Why didn't I put up an archive building of my own? I had many old stories in my mind. Some funny; some poignant; some tragic. All of them trivial and trite perhaps.

And I needed a place to store them. Why didn't I start to build it now while I am still in my early eighties? A man grows old, they tell me, when he approaches ninety.

Take that idea of enjoying God now; a brand new thought. I should certainly file that somewhere—in a place where everybody in the world could see it.

For apparently few people enjoy thinking about God. They are afraid of him. They distrust him. They blame him for everything they dislike, for everything they hate. They profess their utter disbelief in him—and they do away with him by saying, "There is no God." Whisht! Just like that! They pronounce the magic words and God disappears!

The quickness of the hand deceives the eye. The quickness of the hateful heart deceives the mind.

How would you file that in any archive so it wouldn't rust; so it wouldn't gather dust; so time wouldn't yellow it; so it would never lose its freshness; so it would still inspire someone to realize that God is the author of all enjoyment?

If the beginning of wisdom is the fear of the Lord then enjoyment of the Lord is the fullness of wisdom. But how would you phrase it to catch and hold the eye and ear?

"Enjoy God now—now or never?" Or maybe, "Enjoy God and you will enjoy yourself?"

If you enjoy strawberries and apples and pretty girls like Marian and Doreen and perfect June days and riding around the countryside filling your senses with aromatic odors as delicious as those that ascend from the kitchen, then you enjoy God.

The sad point is that maybe you don't realize it *is* God you enjoy and not just the people and things he has made.

"What was the name of the guy who wrote that thing about Katie and the archives?" I asked.

"O'Brien," Marian said. "No, something else. Jones, I think. Maybe Doreen knows. We'll ask her. Is it important?"

"No. Only the guy gave me a good idea. Why don't I start building my own archive building?"

We went out and watched the camel being gassed. That particular camel will run more than a mile for a gallon. But not much more than a mile.

As Marian fastened me into the seat-belt Doreen came

running down her dormitory stairs and climbed into the camel behind my back.

"Who wrote that things about the archives?" I asked her.

"Bill Jakali," she said.

"You didn't hear what I said. I know Bill Jakali is the architect of the archive building. But who's the guy who wrote . . . ."

"Oh him," Doreen said. "Something like Rothchild."

"Thanks," I said, but I didn't really care who wrote what.

I was still blaming myself for neglecting my archive monument. What treasures I had for its tender custody! What characters I had known! What anecdotes I had to tell—if I remembered them!

"You know," I said to Marian as she drove out of the yard, "I have a problem I could easily solve if I had built a place to solve it in."

Marian laughed. "Try the solvation army," she suggested.

I pretended not to enjoy the pun. I pretended I was listening only to the squirrels skirmishing in the pine trees.

"Sorry," she said—in a voice that didn't indicate any measure of sorrow. "What is your problem, Father Eddie?"

"My problem," I said, "is who said it first?"

"Said what first?"

"Yes, that's it." I said.

Solvation army, huh? Let her curiosity squirm a little while. I would enjoy that. She, and Doreen too, I hoped, would enjoy the characters that had just come close to my window—and the perplexing but utterly unimportant problem they brought with them.

"Charley McArthur and Ben Hecht," I said.

The girls were silent waiting for me to go ahead.

"Playwrights," I explained.

"Former newspapermen I worked with in Chicago six hundred years or more ago. They wrote a play about Chicago newspapermen. They called it "The Front Page." There were two stars in the play. One was a reporter called Hildy Johnson. The other was Johnson's city editor. Each of these characters was taken out of real life.

"There was a mutual admiration and respect between them; also a mutual antagonism.

"In the last act the reporter had determined to marry the girl and take her to New York where a real newspaperman belongs; and the city editor was determined to keep him on the staff at any cost.

"There is a sort of reconciliation scene before the reporter leaves the stage for the last time. The editor thanks him for the story he has written and gives him a gold watch as a keepsake.

"That watch is worth a lot of money, he says; but it's worth more than money to me. It was given to me by my staff in Jersey City. See, here's my name engraved on it; to Walter Howey and so forth and so on. I would have put your name on it too but there wasn't time. Anyway, I want you to keep my name close to you.

"The editor stays on his feet a long time after the reporter exits. Nothing is said. Nobody in the audience stirs. Everybody waits to see what the man will do; what he will say."

"What does he say?" Doreen demanded coming as close as she could from the back seat.

"And what does he do?" Marian asked.

"He sits in his swivel chair and talks into the phone. 'Get me the Detective Bureau,' he says. When he has the chief on the line he says, 'Jack, you know Hildy Johnson. I got a tip he's taking the Twentieth Century to New York. I don't want him to get away. The dirty little so-and-so stole my watch.' "

"That was mean," Doreen said.

"And cruel," Marian added. "The poor boy just starting on his honeymoon! Cruel! And what a filthy lie!"

"He got his star reporter back," I pointed out. "And he showed a bit of genius in the process, don't you think?"

"Never mind what we think," Marian said. "Now what was this problem you wanted us to help you solve?"

"Oh that," I said. "I gave that to the solvation army. But let me tell you about two other friends of mine. A married couple. Florabel and Denny. Newspaper people. Big shots, both of them. A few years ago—"

"In the thirteenth or fourteenth century," Doreen interrupted.

"They were driving across the desert. It was getting dark and Florabel was tired. 'Denny,' she said, 'you take the wheel from here to Flagstaff. I'll get out and exercise the dogs.' Denny woke up, waited until his wife and the beagles got out, then snuggled behind the wheel. He was still half asleep when he heard the car door slam shut. He was off and gone the next moment.

"You can imagine how Florabel felt when she returned with the dogs and couldn't see Denny or the car. She was some miles east of Albuquerque. She had no money. She didn't have a friend in that part of the world. What was she going to do?"

"What?" Marian asked. "What?" echoed Doreen.

"Fortunately," I said, "she saw a car approaching. She flagged it down with the help of the dogs and got a ride into Albuquerque. There she went to a newspaper office, identified herself, borrowed some money and asked to use the phone."

"To call a friend?" Marian asked.

"To call the police in Holbrook, Winslow, and Flagstaff. 'Arrest and detain a man named Dennis Morrison,' she said. 'The dirty so-and-so stole my car and everything in it. You got a pencil handy? Here's the license number. I want that man held until I get there.' "

"Wuff," Marian said. "Now I know your problem. Did your playwright friends think of it first or did they adapt it from Florabel and Denny?"

"Or," said Doreen, "did Florabel get the idea from the play?" "Yeah," I said. "If I had my archives in order I would know whether Florabel's act preceded or followed the play."

And, I thought, why didn't I install a chapel in my archive building with an altar on which I could say mass for all my friends, the living and the dead?

And all my enemies!

And all the pitiful people in the world who never enjoyed God and possibly never will?

I made a brave attempt to open the desert window that looks on heaven so I could take the matter directly to headquarters. But—I might have known—it still sticks so tightly in its place I couldn't budge it.

Still, I can talk through that window!

And that is a million times more sensible and profitable than talking through my hat.

22

MY BROTHERS FRANK AND JIM

My brother Frank is dying; and I never knew until I heard the news how much he means to me; how much he meant to me through all his many years. I have said many masses for him and for his intentions and for his family. Also I have said many prayers for him and his.

But I have not asked the Lord to lengthen his days. I do not think he would want me to. I am sure he feels, as I do, that if God is really calling him he should be unafraid to answer: "I hear you and I come."

I know he doesn't want to die—at least not right now. That is natural. Even the saints don't want to die too soon no matter how eager they may be to climb God's holy mountain. Death is a natural thing, of course. We shall all die. I will die and so will you. Everybody around us and about us has died, is dying or will die. God made death so that he could give us eternal life. Only through dying can anyone get to heaven. Only by dying can anyone attain undying joy.

I think I envy my brother Frank more than I grieve for his suffering and his approaching end. I envy him as I envied my brother Jim. Jim and Frank were each born on December 22nd. Jim was exactly four years older than Frank—and often he used to speak of his little brother as his "birthday present."

Jim died at the altar of the little chapel in St. Peter's Church in Chicago's Loop. He had gone to his parish church that morning and received communion. He had eaten a hasty breakfast, then hurried to the Loop to spend an hour in adoration before the blessed sacrament. It was Christmas Eve and he was 69 years and two days old.

It was like Jim to eat his breakfast in a hurry. He was always in a hurry. He was always impatient to get things done. It was like him to run up the stairs of the L station so he could catch the first train going downtown. He didn't want to be late for the "holy hour."

It was like him to run up the stairs from the subway station in the Loop and to rush to the church two blocks away. He wanted to get there in time to ride up to the chapel in the elevator. That little contraption could hold only one or two of the Franciscan monks. Consequently it was seldom used. It ran up from the back of the church every hour on the hour. If you missed it you had to walk up four or five or six or seven—I've forgotten how many—flights of stairs. Jim missed by a few seconds that morning. So he ran up all those terrible narrow steps. The doctors had warned him against climbing too swiftly. But who cared about doctors at a time like this? He was late for his date with Christ. So he had to hurry, didn't he? Let the doctors keep their noses out of this. Jim had made a holy hour every day for years. He knew those stairs.

He got to the chapel. He knelt in adoration. He slumped to the floor. A priest saw him, knew he was dying, and gave him the last rites of the Church. Then he called to a priest downstairs: "Jim Doherty just died. Say the mass for him." Kathleen and Eileen, my sisters, called me an hour or so later saying, "Jim's just gone to heaven."

Jim was a fighter. Jim smashed doors when civic or state

or federal authorities tried to hide from him in the sanctity of their offices.

Jim was, I think, the best reporter in Chicago. He used to stand, five days a week from noon to one o'clock, on the northwest corner of Clark and Randolph Streets for the convenience of his friends. A dozen or more men talked to him during that hour, giving him stories which they would give no other reporter, or giving him tips and hints on stories. When a stranger asked him, "How come you stand there every day and do nothing for a whole hour?" he answered, "Part of my job. Got to see that the Democrats don't steal the City Hall."

Jim was quick to anger; quick to contrition. A word, a look, a gesture could enrage him. And he would be serene and forgiving the next moment. He spent most of his free time getting unfortunate friends out of jail or getting jobs for them. It was fitting for him to die like that.

Frank was a great reporter too. He was also a fighter but I don't believe he ever used his fists. If he did I never heard of it. He took life easy. He was always pleasant, always patient and—like Jim—always ready to help somebody, anybody—even his enemies.

"He gets weaker and weaker," my sisters have reported, "but he keeps fighting even though he may think it's hopeless. He is as cheerful as ever. And he's not afraid. He appreciates the fact that nobody in Chicago has more people praying for him than he has. If he goes to heaven from this hospital, he will go as happily as Jim did."

The other day I was talking about Frank to the Lord. I was speaking through the window that still sticks. Sometimes I can talk through its frosted surface and sometimes I can hear messages coming from it.

I was talking about Frank when I was told to look through the window behind me—the window that looks on the crazy path my pigeon-toed feet have made through the sands and mud puddles and cactus beds of this oasis.

And immediately I was spending a few days of our honeymoon—Catherine's and mine—at a lake resort in Wisconsin.

What was it I was supposed to see? The muskellunge? Probably not.

A woman in a cabin close to ours caught a tremendous specimen. She was sitting on her pier fishing for minnows which her husband might use for bait. He was far away with a party of old fishermen trolling for nothing but "muskies." The fish headed right onto her hook and into her landing net; and we had part of him for supper. I liked it. That astonished Catherine.

"So," she said, "I'm going to cook a fish for you every Friday."

"O.K.," I said, "but only a muskellunge." (So I never got fish on Friday.)

Maybe I was to take another look at the slot machine? We hadn't enough money to take us home. Catherine had met some poor families. To us a poor family was always a good excuse for spending money.

"Give me a quarter," she said. She put the coin into a slot machine, turned a handle and churned up three lemons in a row—and the machine spat a hundred or more quarters into her lap. No, that was not important.

Oh. Now I know. The soldier. The soldier, of course! How nice of God to remind me of him.

It was Sunday and we were at high mass in the local church. The soldier was young, tall, and slender. There were ribbons on his tunic that indicated medals he had won in battle. That boy had seen the face of death so close it could have kissed him.

I lifted my eyes from his ribbons to his face. And I saw the face of a saint. He was coming from the communion rail and Catherine and I were going toward it. We both stood a moment actually staring at him. He had had not only a close-up of death, he had also enjoyed a close-up of eternal life! His face, I thought, might have been the shining face of Christ.

I envied him. Desperately I envied him. I had, sometime before our marriage, decided to be a saint. Come hell or high water, as we catholics say, I was going to be a saint! I owed that to God. And to Catherine—and to all her kids in Friendship House.

Here was a hero home from the wars who made me look like a two-bit mediocre marshmallow holy Joe!

I knew I should never shine that way with the love of God. I would never feel anything like the rapture that kid showed to the world around him. I wasn't his kind. I had no special fervor for God. I didn't like praying on my knees. I never spent more time at the altar than I was supposed to—or was forced to. I felt closer to Got out in the country than I did in a cathedral. I had actually fled from some.

How was I going to be a saint if I didn't love God enough? Someone came to my help. Blessed Martin de Porres maybe, or St. Therese, the "little flower," perhaps even St. Joseph, or Our Lady herself.

"Nobody loves God enough. Nobody can. So what I want you to do is to love everybody God has made—even the least of Christ's brethren."

"Love your friends. Love your enemies. Love Catherine. Love the boys and girls in Friendship House. (This was long before there was a Madonna House to love.) Love people you don't even like. Love the bores who want to tell you all their woes. Love the people who borrow your money or your books and never return either. Love all the shy and bashful and awkward and lonely and frightened people you touch. Remember, a kiss can be a prayer."

I remembered a church in a small town in Italy where I found some brown habited nuns teaching little children to blow kisses to the altar.

"Every kiss should be a prayer," I thought. "Why can't every prayer become a kiss? Suppose I intend it that way and leave the rest to the Lord!"

Jim and Frank once wore uniforms. During the first world war Jim was a soldier; and Frank was a sailor.

Maybe Jim's face shone like that as he lay there in the chapel in the Loop looking up at the host in the golden monstrance and at all the angelic candle flames around it.

Maybe Frank's face too will shine like that before the priest or the nurse or the doctor closes his eyes. It wouldn't surprise me.

It doesn't surprise me that he takes so long. Even as a child he was patient. Life was good to him. It gave him his wife Mary. It gave him fine children. It gave him grandchildren. It gave him happiness. It gave him abundant love.

He and Mary have had a longer honeymoon than Catherine and I. Frank has always loved the Church. So

God has given him a long time to prepare for the life to come.

He took this life easy, as the saying goes. He will take the next life easy too.

When it's my time you and Jim can help me up that mountain. How often have you met me at the railroad station or the airport to help me with my luggage and to take me home in your car? I expect to meet you when I come. Bring Jim with you if he's not arguing politics with some Democratic saint or religion with some holy protestant.

And hey, while I think of it, why not bring the whole gang with you?

How wonderful a man's death can be!

A man's death can bring splendor as well as sorrow to all who knew him.

So long, Frankie boy. God love you forever. See you soon.

23

WHY SHOULD I MOURN?

Six candles stood on the altar as Father Briere and I said mass for my brother Frank who had died the day before on the eve of the feast of the Immaculate Conception, just as I had finished writing about him.

This was on December 8th in our own Madonna House Chapel of the Immaculate Conception of Our Lady in Combermere.

There were six candles but only two were lighted; and that to me was most significant. There had been six boys in our family and five girls. Six boys and two had died. Six candles and only two were shining brightly before the Lord.

"We are all candles," I thought. "We are not all wax nor all tallow, but everyone of us has a wick—a soul—that can be ignited by the love of God or of our neighbors and burn until the candle is consumed."

"We should burn as brightly all our lives as these two do now. Must it be only in our deaths that we reveal the flames that kill us?"

We had breakfast after mass and Ray Gene Neubig, one of our staff nurses, was appointed to go with me to Chicago where the funeral would be held and then on to this oasis in Arizona where my doctors and nurses want me to spend the winter.

We drove through dim gray light, spates of rain and spatters of snow, two hundred miles or so to Toronto. There we boarded a plane for Chicago. And all the time I kept thinking of the mystery of the candles.

As the plane neared Chicago I found myself coming closer and closer, not to the dead Frank, but to Frank alive and well and smiling as I always saw him. As usual he would be waiting at the airport for me. He would insist on carrying the luggage. He would drive me to the house on Sawyer Avenue. He would have dinner with us—even if it were only a cup of coffee before he went to his own home.

"I miss him," I said to Ray Gene. When you miss someone you love, you find him. He is with you and dearer than you realized. You may never see him again but you will never be far away from him so long as you live.

He wasn't waiting for me at the airport. Yet he was most certainly there. A candle gleams more brightly in the dark hours than it does in the light.

We got a taxi and the driver thought he knew Chicago better than I did. He chose his own way to our old home in Sawyer Avenue. Frank rode with us, whispering snide but funny remarks about the chauffeur. Frank was the gentlest and the most loving of all the Doherty boys; and the things he said were seldom meant to hurt.

Marty was at the house when we arrived—the Reverend Martin W. Doherty, pastor emeritus of St. Mary's Church in Albany, Oregon, referred to usually as "our bachelor priest." (This, to distinguish him from me.)

And Bill was there, my brother from Los Alamitos, California, and Tom, and my sisters Kathleen and Eileen.

Tom and the girls live in the downstairs flat and rent the upstairs to tenants.

Six of us—seven with Ray Gene—sat around the dinner table. "Oh, I know you had something to eat on the plane but you can take a cup of coffee or tea and maybe a piece of fruit cake." Six of the eleven children. Six candles. Each waiting for the altar boy to come out from the sacristy and set them afire.

Immediately Frank strolled into the room smiling that gentle warming smile as he greeted us. This wasn't any ordinary meal. This was one of the old "gatherings of the clan," one of the family reunions we had when we were eight, and not yet six.

Every year on November 20th, the anniversary of our parents' wedding day, we would get together if we could, no matter how far apart we might be, and celebrate the event with a lobster dinner. Sometimes we went to a restaurant. Sometimes we stayed home in this house on Sawyer Avenue, in this very room and had the food delivered.

Now if I were the sort of man who remembered things he ate I might report exactly all we devoured on these happy evenings. I will do my best but I am sure to leave something out. Forgive me.

First, naturally, there would be a mound of steamed clams for each of us. And warm clam broth. And some kind of goo to dip the clams in if you wanted to. There would be clusters of shining black ripe olives still in their mother's oil. There would be a lettuce and tomato salad, infiltrated with chunks of soft and really mature Roquefort cheese. There would be slices of garlic bread anointed with soft unsalted butter. There would be great bowls of shoestring potatoes, warm, limp, and blessed with the fragrance of butter fresh from the churn.

Then, the lobsters themselves in all their scarlet glory. Gracious vessels filled with golden molten butter. Big fresh lemons to squeeze on the lobster meat. And hot black coffee.

Jim could put away half a dozen lobsters. Frank could never manage more than two. (Neither could I.) Tom and Bill were almost as stalwart eaters as Jim.

Tom always wanted pie and ice cream to finish the meal. The girls were dainty. They talked rather than ate as they watched us work.

Frank always pretended he wanted to pay for the dinner or his share of it. He had no more intention than I had to do anything of the kind. He merely wanted to tease Jim. Jim never took Frank seriously but he hushed him just the same. Jim always paid. Jim was always "throwing parties." Jim was always giving away money, especially to his nephews and nieces. Jim was always making life easier for someone.

I came into Chicago one day to find him in a room in the Sherman hotel. He was at the phone. Evidently he had ordered dinner for a big crowd of his friends. I got there in time to hear him order the "refreshments."

"One case of scotch, the best you got. One case of bourbon. One case of rye. One case of Burgundy. One case of champagne. No, dammit of course not. No imported wines for us. We got better stuff here than anywhere in Europe. Make it a case of Imperial from California. Yeah, that's all. No, wait. Four bottles of Coca-cola. For me."

He explained he had won more than $2500 that morning in the daily double and he was throwing a party for his friends on the Chicago Tribune.

Jim and Frank were with us six and with "Nurse Pe," my brother Tom's name for Ray Gene. And weren't the clams and the lobsters good! And the shoestring potatoes! And the garlic bread! Best of all was watching Tom, little

Tommy then—put away that apple pie a la mode.

I managed to get to the funeral parlor—a ghastly place—and to stay awhile to meet friends I hadn't seen in years and relatives I scarcely recognized. But I couldn't stay long. Frank's body was there; and his widow and his children and maybe some of his grandchildren. But Frankie wasn't there. I had to get out of the place.

The weather was bad. It was worse the next day and it continued to get worse. Ray Gene wouldn't let me out of bed except to say a Byzantine mass for Frank and to concelebrate with Marty in a Latin-rite mass.

I was not allowed to return to the funeral parlor. I was not permitted to go to the church nor to escort the body to Calvary—where he was buried, not too far from Jim, not too far from his parents, not too far from his sisters, not too far from his sisters-in-law, my wives, Marie and Mildred.

My bed became my poustinia, my oasis in the desert. I spent the hours there peering through the window that looks upon the lights and shadows of my past. I couldn't see anything. I wasn't hungry enough even to nibble at the past. And there was that voice that kept demanding my attention.

"Life isn't just "eat, drink, and be merry." Nor is it "eat, drink, and be buried." Life is a love affair with God. Too often it is only God who loves. The good die young? Why shouldn't the old die good?"

The voice was coming through the clouds that blinded the window meant to open on heaven, the one that always sticks, the stubborn, unyielding, baffling portal that has never given me even a glimpse of God nor of his mother nor of any of his saints or angels.

I sat up and listened.

"Do not talk of candles, lit or unlit—and especially of candles only half lit. Talk of stars. Talk of the star of Bethlehem so bright it brought the Magi riding from their homes so many hundreds of miles away; the star that brought them to the altar of the new born king.

"The Magi adored their king and their God and gave him costly treasures. They gave him everything but themselves. Give him yourself.

"Let the star of Bethlehen shine in your heart—and in the hearts of all the people you know and love. Let it shine brightly so that millions and millions of modern Magi may come to adore him.

"Why light a candle when you can light a star?"

I got out of bed to write what I had heard—in rough notes which I will have trouble reading when I find them. I never fail to get out of bed for this purpose except when I am too lazy or too sleepy or too certain that I will not forget. I got up and scribbled notes on the back of an envelope.

But the voice resumed its lecture when I slithered back into the sheets beneath the electric blanket.

"And don't forget the tide," the voice said.

"What tide?" I wondered.

"The ebb tide. The shining red tide that poured out of the great flood gates into the Mediterranean Sea."

Of course I had forgotten that tide. I had forgotten it, I imagine, because it had no particular meaning at the time. It was a dream. Ray Gene's dream. She remembered enough of it to relate it.

"I dreamed I was in the Holy Land on a visit. Theresa Davis was in Jerusalem. Mary Davis was in Nazareth.

Susan Adams was the only Madonna House staff worker in our house at Haifa and she was giving me a tour of the place. She took me first to the archbishop's palace. I had heard so much about it. It was a shabby, tumble-down, moldy, old place, a piece of junk. But the court or patio was splendid. With beautiful walks and date palms and olive trees and many flowers and a great wide round pool.

"Archbishop Raya and Father Eddie are singing the divine liturgy in the pool," Susan said. 'We can't disturb them now so let me show you the rest of the place.'

"We went all over the city and finally we came to a great wide stream and a tremendous pair of flood gates. As I watched, the gates opened and a torrent of wine poured out into the rising sunlight into the sea."

" 'That's the blood of Jesus consecrated by Father Eddie and the archbishop ebbing into the ocean—to sanctify and sweeten all the world,' Susan explained."

I lay in bed a long time thinking of that blessed and beautiful tide pouring out of the gates of time into the sea of eternity.

Finally the message was clear. Marty and I and many other priests had said masses for Frank before and after he died. And all his friends had prayed for him and had masses offered for him.

One of the last things he said was, "Why don't they let me alone so I can go to heaven?"

He had gone to heaven in glory, his soul floating in the ebb tide of God's eternal love.

Why should I mourn for him?

24

LADY AT THE GOLDEN DOOR

Once upon a time—really a very recent time—I heard a bell ringing just outside my homemade desert cell. And, slave to bells that I am, I left whatever I was doing and all my worldly goods—including three examples of petrified wood—and hurried to partake of dinner and discussion. You know, chit-chat and chitlings—and maybe chicken leftovers too.

Catherine, here in Arizona on visitation with Father Briere, and all the girls of the Casa were already seated around the table waiting for the blessing.

While the food was being knife-and-forked and guzzled and forgotten, Catherine began to speak of her love for Arizona and for all the United States of America and for Americans in general.

Father Briere, born and bred in Canada, said he too loved America and Americans and somebody proved that by reading a piece he wrote for *Restoration* a few months ago. In that lovely essay Father Briere informally canonized Martin Luther King, Jr., President John F. Kennedy, and the president's brother, Robert Kennedy. The staff workers, Canadian and American, joined the chorus of praise. And I said nothing. Nothing at all.

Why is it you forget the chitlings as soon as they pass your palate on the way down, while the chit-chat may remain forever in your mind? Maybe it is because food for the body is nothing like food for the soul. (A fellow remembers with delight, naturally, such things as lobster tails in melted butter, the first taste of real caviar on thin hot potato pancakes, the last cup of Turkish coffee, and other things eaten and drunk at various times.) But these are shadows of the past, whereas some chit-chat is all substance and no shadow.

I went eventually back to my deserted desert, played with the petrified wood awhile, and began looking out the window of my past.

A woman came close to the window, a pleasant, smiling, admiring woman. I had no idea who she was until she spoke. Then I recognized her.

"Aren't you proud to be an American?" she asked.

She was the lady who owned and ran the only drugstore in the litle Finnish town of Rovaniemi where so many of us war correspondents were quartered during the first few months of 1940, during the "sit-down" period of the second world war.

"I don't mean you are proud because America is such a mighty nation," she continued. "I mean you should be proud because America is such a magnificent nation, such a wonderful nation, such a peace-loving nation, such a merciful nation."

"Whenever there is a great catastrophe in some part of the world, a plague, an earthquake, a tidal wave, devastating fire, a tremendous famine, American ships come steaming in loaded with foods, medicines, and doctors and nurses, and men and women who want to stay and help. Wherever there is dire poverty, American dollars come singing the mercy of God. Wherever there is aggression, American troops come ashore to keep the people free."

It was the first time I had seen my country through

foreign eyes. It was the first time, I think, that I realized
how very much I loved my nature land, my very own people.

The Russian planes had passed over Rovaniemi in the
north of the country a dozen times but they had never
dropped any bombs. I stood out in the open now and then,
and listened to their thunder. Once their bombs fell far
away. None of them touched us. The only thing that
happened that particular day was that a reindeer twitched
his ears. It was the day before my visa expired and I had to
leave. I went to Sweden and thence to France and from
there to Genoa, Italy, where I learned I could get a ship for
New York. In Sweden I met an English correspondent fresh
from Finland who was hurrying back to England. He was
shaking so much he could neither light a cigarette nor lift
his cup from the table.

"They bombed Rovaniemi at last," he said, "and I
couldn't take it. Back to England for me. If they bomb us, I
think I'll kill myself. You remember that lady who owned
the drugstore, the pretty one who spoke such perfect
English? I saw her lying outside the store with her two
daughters. The bomb had taken her head off. Why
couldn't you Yankees have done something for the Finns?"

I kept hearing the voices of Catherine and Father Briere.
I kept remembering things Catherine had said about
America when I first met her—in that same year of 1940.

She had loved Abe Lincoln ever since she had read about
him, and his love for the slaves, and for all mankind.
"Charity for all," she liked to quote. "Malice toward
none." And she loved the words of Emma Lazarus
engraved on the Statue of Liberty. "Give me your tired,
your poor; your huddled masses yearning to breathe free.

The wretched refuse of your teeming shore; send them to me. I lift my lamp beside the golden door."

I have looked at that statue hundreds of times and always with emotion. In my early days as a newspaperman in New York I was often sent out to meet some incoming liner to interview some world celebrity aboard. And at such times I spent hours looking at some of the humbler passengers as they passed the statue. Some of them wept at the sight. Some of them embraced and kissed and danced as though they had seen the hand of Our Lady or Our Lord and has been forever blessed.

In the year of 1919 I was sent by the Chicago Tribune to welcome the Illinois troops coming home from Europe. Early one morning another reporter and I hired a motor boat to take us out to the fleet which was anchored in the bay awaiting the sunrise to come in. We wanted exclusive interviews for our papers. We were sincerely and joyously welcomed—the first American civilians those boys had seen in two years. And how they laughed at our straw hats!

We passed the Statue of Liberty in the full splendor of the dawn.

"There she is," one boy said. "The old girl herself."

There were hundreds of others there. Maybe thousands. None of them said a single word. But I wish I could show you the way each one looked at that beautiful lady who lifted her lamp beside the golden door.

Lots of people love America, I thought. But nobody loves the country more than those Americans who have left it for a time and have at last come back to it.

I drifted off to sleep finally and somehow Our Lady got mixed up in my dreams and my memories and my emotions. She was the Lady with the lamp lifted high above the golden door.

She was the great lover of America and Americans—a nation and a people dedicated to her Immaculate Conception. She was the Lady holding a light to guard all the tired, the poor, the homeless, the tempest-tossed, the refuse of our teeming shores, into the coziness and the warmth and the shelter and the love of the palace of her father and her son and her holy spouse.

May is her month. But she lifts the lamp in June, July, August, September, October, November, December, January, February, March and April. Hail Mary, full of grace! Hail Lady of the lamp! Pray for us now and at the hour of darkness when we need the light to see the way home.